DEAKIN   JULY 200...

Vis...
N...

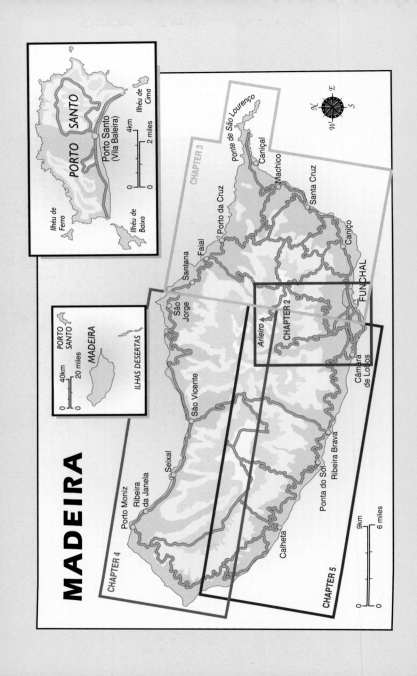

VISITOR'S GUIDE
MADEIRA

Jutta May

walks by
Susanne Lipps

MPC

Published in the USA by:
Hunter Publishing Inc,
300 Raritan Center Parkway,
CN 94, Edison, NJ 08818

Published by:
Moorland Publishing Co Ltd,
Moor Farm Road West, Ashbourne,
Derbyshire DE6 1HD England

ISBN 0 86190 533 4

© Goldstadtverlag Karl A. Schäfer, Pforzheim

© Moorland Publishing Co Ltd 1994 (English Edition)
Reprinted with amendments, 1996

British Library Cataloguing in Publication Data:
A catalogue record for this book is available from the British Library.

Colour origination by: Forest Graphics Ltd, Nottingham & GA Graphics,
Stamford, Lincolnshire

Printed in Hong Kong by: Wing King Tong Co Ltd

Cover photograph: Santana
Rear Cover: (left) Ribeira Brava from Miradouro, (middle) Pointsettia,
(right) View from Pico do Arieiro, (below) Ribeira Frias
Page 3: Cabo Girão from Levada dos Piornais *(All MPC Picture Collection)*

All illustrations are from the MPC Picture Collection

Translated by: Paul Fletcher

MPC Production Team:
Editorial, design and additional text: John Robey
Cartography: Alastair Morrison

While every care has been taken to ensure that the information in this
book is as accurate as possible at the time of publication, the publisher
and authors accept no responsibility for any loss, injury or inconven-
ience sustained by anyone using this book.

CONTENTS

Key to Symbols Used in Text Margin and on Maps

🚶 Recommended walks   ⛪ Church

🌻 Garden   🎴 Building of interest

🏰 Castle/Fortification   �w Viewpoint *(miradouro)*

⛵ Water sports/boat trip   🏛 Museum/Art Gallery

Key to Colour Maps

———— Main Road   City

———— Secondary Road   ◯ Town /Village

———— Minor Road   River

Key to Walk Maps

B Bus stop   ✳ Point of interest

T Taxistand   ⛪ Church

H Hotel   ■ Building

R Restaurant   �w Viewpoint *(miradouro)*

B Bar   🌻 Garden

M Mountain hut   ▲ Peak

How To Use This Guide

This MPC Visitor's Guide has been designed to be as easy to use as possible. Each chapter covers a region or itinerary in a natural progression which gives all the background information to help you enjoy your visit. MPC's distinctive margin symbols, the important places printed in bold, and a comprehensive index enable the reader to find the most interesting places to visit with ease.

At the end of each chapter an Additional Information section gives specific details such as addresses and opening times, making this guide a complete sightseeing companion.

At the back of the guide the Fact File, arranged in alphabetical order, gives practical information and useful tips to help you plan your holiday before you go and while you are there.

The maps of each region show the main towns, villages, roads, and places of interest, but are not designed as route maps and motorists should always use a good recommended road atlas.

INTRODUCTION

Surrounded by the waters of the Atlantic, but close to the African coast Madeira enjoys a climate where colourful flowers thrive and magnificent wine is produced. It is an island founded on rocks and its original inhabitants came from Portugal about 500 years ago. They called themselves 'Madeirans', created a well ordered society, acquiring a reputation for hard work and warm hospitality. They produce the world-famous madeira wine, marvellous embroidery and in modern times their sunny island has become a haven for northern Europeans who find there all the comforts that they could wish for, set in spectacular mountain scenery.

The shores of the neighbouring island of Porto Santo provide the only good beaches, but there are countless freshwater and saltwater swimming pools so that bathers do not have to forego their daily dip.

Tennis courts abound and watersports on offer include snorkelling, water-skiing and windsurfing, but with level ground being at a premium there are only two golf courses. In many areas, tracks and footpaths have been improved to give walkers and mountain-climbers access to the hinterland. A modern casino offers gamblers another opportunity to make their fortune. Other popular pursuits include trout fishing, deep-sea fishing or deep-sea diving. Delight the palate with tasty Madeiran fare and grace the nose with the fragrance of the flowers — or the wine! Lovers of art and architecture will find many examples of the Portuguese Manueline style in all its subtle beauty.

The Discovery of Madeira

Lying in the Atlantic Ocean, 606km (380 miles) west of Morocco and 416km (260 miles) north of the Canary Islands, the island of Madeira was unknown to Europeans until the fifteenth century, when two Portuguese sailors sought refuge on nearby Porto Santo after being blown off course during a storm. The explorers had no idea that a further 37km (23miles) to the south-west lay an even bigger island which had the added benefit of plentiful fresh water.

Blown off course again in 1418, they saw from a distance the reality of what they had earlier taken to be a mirage. A year later the two explorers, João Gonçalves Zarco and Tristão Vaz Texeira, finally went ashore and decided to give the tree-covered island the name 'Madeira', meaning 'wood'. This green, fertile, uninhabited landscape was blessed with countless streams and rivers splashing down the hillsides. In many of the places where these watercourses flowed into the sea lay small shingly plateaux, but if the explorers envisaged settling here, then there was space for little more than a few houses. The greatest expanse of suitable terrain was to be found at the site of what is now the island's capital, Funchal, but even that was barely sufficient. The only other extensive flat area was not found until later. It lies high up in the mountains but consists largely of marshland (Paúl da Serra).

Initially more and more of the woodland around the first simple settlements was cleared away, partly for the construction of homes and partly for boatbuilding, but the land which was recovered from tree-felling was too rocky or too steep to be developed for habitation or agricultural use. The resourceful islanders soon devised a way of putting these inhospitable slopes to good use — terraces. Surrounding the small settlements like an amphitheatre, these terraces were later to yield a crop that was to bring wealth and fame to the island. Once again good fortune played an important part. By resorting to fire to clear away the otherwise worthless bushes and trees, the settlers were unaware that the residual ashes had given the soil a special richness.

Water, however, plays the most important part in creating sustainable farmland and there was plenty of it, but unfortunately not where it was needed. It was this unavoidable geographical fact that led to the construction of the *levadas*. Years of backbreaking work went into channelling natural watercourses and creating a network of artificial riverlets and canals across the island, through the mountains, along the hillsides and into practically every field. A cleverly designed system was devised so that at a given time a given quantity of water could be supplied to almost every plot of land. In later years the *levadas* came under government control and they are now carefully regulated. Paths run alongside the channels so that the watercourses can be maintained and many of these have become the footpaths enjoyed by today's walkers. The latest *levada* (from Monte above Funchal to Santa Cruz on the east coast) was built in the 1960s, extends for about 100km (60miles) and includes several sections of tunnel.

For the visitor, the green and flourishing chequerboard of fields dotted with small, thatched *palheiros* or cowsheds makes an attractive sight. The Madeiran may have a different perspective faced with the daunting prospect of cultivating every possible square yard of steeply sloping land. Beyond, however, jagged rocky peaks dominate the island and these symbolise the indomitable spirit of the hard-working islanders.

The Landscape of Madeira

Madeira covers 741sq km (281sq miles), which represents about one third of the area of Luxembourg. The island measures just 57km (35miles) in length and 22.5km (14miles) in width. The highest peak reaches 1,861m (6,100ft), but it rises up from 4,000m (13,120ft) beneath the sea. Tremendous forces within the earth's core threw up massive mountain ranges and a series of volcanoes, and the greatest mountain range in the world, 16,000km (9,900miles) long and 800km (500miles) wide, extends across the floor of the Atlantic. Its height averages 3,000m (9,900ft) or about 1,500m (4,900ft) below sea-level. The Azores form the highest peaks of this mountain range with the Pico Alto rising 8,400m (27,500ft) above the sea bottom but only 2,320m (7,610ft) above sea-level. Between these underwater mountain ranges and the shelf off west Africa lies the Cape Verde Basin where the ocean floor descends to more than 7,000m (23,000ft). At the eastern edge, close to the African shelf, the archipelagos of Madeira and the Canary Islands have emerged from the ocean.

The rocky ridges with their steep sides and the deep valleys or *ribeiras* bear witness both to the island's volcanic origins and the ensuing forces of erosion. The interplay of colour between the dark basalt and lava and the bright red volcanic slag and ash layers, interspersed with the yellowish tufa and its covering of generally lush vegetation combine to create a landscape which is reminiscent of the Dolomites or even the Black Forest. In contrast in the barren, sometimes marshy and misty plateau of Paúl da Serra, the visitor may well feel himself transported to northern Scotland.

Around 100 million years ago a volcanic eruption 4,000m (13,000ft) below sea-level created the core of the mountain range. It was only 10 million years ago that the island emerged from the sea and a number of fossils, found mainly on the neighbouring island of

The contrasting Madeiran landscape — lush vegetation reaching high into the mountains near São Vicente, and (opposite) cliffs of volcanic ash at Ponta do Pargo at the westernmost point of the island

Porto Santo, date from around this time. In the following years a chain of volcanic islands similar to Hawaii formed, much bigger in overall size than now, but the forces of erosion have been chipping away incessantly at the volcanic rock ever since. Rainwater furrowed the sides of the mountains and washed the often loose stones into the sea. Atlantic waves have pounded the shores to create the steep cliff-faces, now such a distinctive feature of the island. Today, Madeira is a volcanic relic, almost certainly extinct as there have been no further eruptions in the recorded past.

The slopes in the north of the island are steeper with many water-falls cascading from the near vertical hillsides. The northern coast is wetter and nearly always cooler than the southern side of the island, where the hillsides tend to fall gently down to the sea, creating at the same time an often inaccessible and rocky shoreline. The few pebbly beaches are small and the dry hinterland requires artificial irrigation in order to create worthwhile agricultural land.

Madeirans are not impressed by claims that their island is all that remains of the sunken continent of Atlantis. It is even said by some, perhaps not surprisingly, that the island is all that is left of paradise on earth. For the islanders, Madeira is not a relic or a leftover and they point repeatedly to the important role bestowed on the island by Diaz, Columbus, Vasco da Gama and Magellan who all used the Atlantic island as a staging post on their Voyages of Discovery — the Madeirans are quick to claim their share in the glory. Similarly, in the seventeenth century, the island became an important base and supply station for British vessels engaged in trade with west Africa.

The History of Madeira

Was it simply good fortune that Madeira was discovered or was it bound to happen? Fortune certainly smiled on the aristocrats of eighteenth-century Europe. How else would they have found the 'finest wine on earth' had the Madeirans not first obtained the secret from Crete and then used the plentiful sun and their own hard work to produce it?

It had been the idea of Henry the Navigator (1394-1460) who was charged by the Portuguese court with the task of developing the island's economy. He also imported sugar cane from Sicily. By 1452, the first sugar mill on Madeira was in operation and before long so much of the sweet substance had reached Europe that even the common man could afford it.

Henry's father, João I (1385-1433), an illegitimate son of King Pedro I and former Grand Master of the Avis order, founded Portugal's new Avis dynasty. João's half-brother, Fernando, who had followed Pedro to the throne, sought to create the union of two kingdoms by marrying his daughter to John of Castile. This union proved unpopular with the Portuguese people and their victory over the invading Castilian army in 1385 brought independence to Portugal and João to the throne. He was responsible for a period of prosperity, continued the internal reforms initiated by his father Pedro I and secured the support of the English court. Shipbuilding and trade thrived and with the defeat in 1415 of the Moroccan trading and pirate base of Ceuta, he created a climate in which Portugal's colonial aspirations could flourish.

João's youngest son, Henry the Navigator, was devoted to the sea and to a large extent he provided the impetus for the great Voyages of Discovery. The invention of the compass, the recognition of the fact that the world was round and the establishment by Henry of an observatory and a school for geography and navigation (with maritime warfare also a subject for study), all laid the foundations for the exploration of the world.

In fact as early as 1200BC the Phoenicians had passed through the 'Pillars of Hercules' (Gibraltar) but they did not reveal what they found beyond. Greek and Roman cartographers are agreed about the existence of the Canary Islands, but it was the fourteenth century before these islands were re-discovered. One chart from this period even mentions an 'Island of Wood' but it must have been forgotten until Henry the Navigator and his mariners put it back on the map and brought the island to people's attention.

In 1440 Henry granted coastal towns to each of the island's discoverers as hereditary fiefdoms. Zarco received Funchal which was already developing as a settlement, Texeira assumed responsibility for Machico and Bartolomeu Perestrelo for the island of Porto Santo. Their powers also included authority over the immediate hinterland.

But scarcely fifty years later, the enlightened administration of the island by the discoverers' heirs incurred the displeasure of Portugal's king, Manuel I, and in 1497 he placed Madeira under the direct rule of the Portuguese crown. In the same year pirates plundered the island, destroying all the ships in the harbour, one of which was carrying building material for Funchal's cathedral. In 1508 King Manuel I declared Funchal the official capital of the Madeiran archipelago.

Columbus visited the island four times. His first three stays were brief and undertaken in his capacity as a sugar trader. On the fourth occasion he stayed longer and married there before beginning his voyage to America in 1492. While living in Funchal, he resided in Rua do Esmeraldo where he became preoccupied with the study of navigation. The house has been demolished but the finely carved window frames were rebuilt in the garden of the Quinta da Palmeira (Levada de Santa Luzia).

In relation to English history, Madeira's strong links with London grew out of the marriage in 1662 between the Portuguese king's daughter, Catharine of Braganza, and the Stuart king, Charles II. Part of the marriage contract involved the Madeirans agreeing to export madeira wine directly to British colonies in north America, thereby bypassing the usual detour via England and any unloading and loading on to English ships.

Such favourable trading conditions, not to mention the agreeable Madeiran climate, attracted many English merchants and their families to the island. Since then Madeira has been home to a sizeable British community.

During the Napoleonic Wars a British force occupied the island to safeguard the port as a revictualling point for the navy and many of the soldiers remained on the island, marrying native girls. So do not be surprised to see blond-haired, blue-eyed Madeirans. The story behind the island's black African population has no such romantic connotations. Their ancestors were brought over from west Africa to work as slaves on the plantations or to perform the most dangerous tasks in the construction of the *levadas* and roads. They were lowered down the rock faces in wicker baskets and left swinging at dizzying heights to clear a way through the hard rock.

Towards the middle and end of the nineteenth century, disaster struck the island. In 1852 and 1873 the vines were afflicted by a deadly disease and in 1873 the sugar cane plants also succumbed. 1856 brought an epidemic of cholera which claimed many lives. It is often maintained that the new vinestocks are not of the same quality as the old ones and the modern madeira wine does not match the prized vintages of the last century. There is now no way of knowing if any difference exists, although today's madeira producers continue to profit from the wine's fine reputation.

Towards the end of the last century at about the same time as disaster struck a new source of income, later to become a thriving industry, was making inroads into the local economy — tourism.

It was mainly English men and women suffering from consumption brought on by the British climate, who were recommended by doctors to recuperate in the soothing and therapeutic mild air this sunlit and wooded island breathed. Sanatoria for those with bronchial complaints were followed by *pensions* and hotels for visiting

Monte Palace — one of the many large houses built by wealthy Madeirans to take advantage of the area's therapeutic climate — the splendid gardens are now open to the public

Portuguese painted tiles or azulejos *are also to be seen on Madeira*

relatives. Whether the floral splendour of Madeira did anything other than put thoughts of illness to one side is not clear, but it certainly enticed many new visitors to the island's shores. Cruise ships anchored off Funchal and the word soon spread that a visit to this beautiful, restful and tranquil island, surrounded by blue sea, together with the warm hospitality of the native people could delight and benefit everyone.

An Architectural Delight

With what is now known as the Manueline style, Madeiran architecture has something special to offer visitors. Named after the Portuguese king, Manuel I (1495-1521), there are only a few examples of the style to be found on the island, but what does exist is unmistakeable. These early years of the sixteenth century have come to be recognised as Portugal's heyday as a colonial and trading nation, although in the final years of Manuel's successor, João III (1521-57), signs of decadence were already evident.

The discovery of Madeira and later the world beyond heralded a new era in Europe. Formerly the Mediterranean basin had been the focus of attention for expansionist rulers, but with Portugal's acquisition of Madeira, for the first time a European country was looking outside the traditional boundaries. Here was a new land, not a colony, but a part of the mother country. Soon after the first settlers arrived, artisans and builders followed. Churches and palaces were built in the same style as those they had built on the mainland, where northern Gothic had blended with southern splendour, converging finally in early Renaissance style. In the Portuguese variation, however, the Voyages of Discovery had contributed certain distinctive features, such as motifs from India.

On the mainland there was a tendency to exaggerate the style with baroque clutter, but on Madeira the decorations were simpler. Only capitals, keystones, window and door frames were decorated. Knowledgeable visitors will immediately recognise the subtle differences, but the most striking feature of the Manueline style on Madeira is the variety of building materials — wood and stone were not the only materials used.

The special geology of the island gave architects and builders access to basalt in colours ranging from grey to bright red, while the delicate tones of the yellowish tufa (related to sandstone) can, when used carefully, lend a special charm. Of the many types of wood available, the delightfully scented cedar was very popular with builders, whether for use in simple timbered ceilings or in carved coffering. Interestingly, Moorish motifs, originating in southern Spain and reaching Madeira via the Portuguese mainland, can often be found. They are almost entirely geometric in form.

Also of Moorish origin are the *azulejos*, enamelled tiles used as decorations and arranged either in lined borders or patterns or combined with scenes to create murals rather like a framed painting. The term 'azulejo' is almost certainly Moorish and is thought to derive from 'al zulaich' meaning small slab or tile. Another theory argues that the first Portuguese examples were blue (*azul*) on white and the word may well just mean 'blue tiles'.

Even though in the course of time many things need to be renewed or simply have to give way to the new order, the interested visitor will still find many fine examples of the country's 'Golden Age', when Portuguese mariners circumnavigated the world, exploring the oceans and distant lands inspiring a unique artistic style which bears the name of Manuel, Portugal's king and which here on Madeira still carries its own special stamp.

Surprisingly, many paintings by Flemish masters have been found, particularly in the churches. As a system of barter was favoured by Dutch traders, the paintings are thought to have found their way to Madeira during the period of sugar exports.

Climate

As an Atlantic island Madeira's climate is understandably subject entirely to the influences of the vast ocean. It lies beyond the cold northern winds and also well away from debilitating tropical heat. The prevailing north-east Trade Winds generally bring fine weather and the Gulf Stream steady warmth. Rain-bearing north-westerlies do, however, affect mainly the north-western side of the island during the winter months and here and up in the mountains, rain is more frequent and heavier than on the south side.

The climate varies almost as much as the landscape. The south coast receives some 550mm (22in) of rainfall a year and average maximum daytime temperatures vary between 18°C/64°F in winter and 25°C/77°F in summer, thus creating a very pleasant year-round climate. In the central highlands, rainfall can amount to 3,000mm (120in), winter temperatures sink to about 5°C/40°F and conditions can be none too agreeable, with mists often enveloping the higher peaks during the winter months. Precipitation on the north coast is usually higher than on the south side and the temperature a few degrees lower. The proximity of the sea generally helps to create a climate without too many extremes and at any time of the year, there are certain to be days of uninterrupted sunshine, even on the mountain tops. Given the varying climatic conditions on Madeira, there is always likely to be somewhere free of rain and cloud, somewhere for the walker to enjoy. The south and east sides of the island are recommended for the winter, while in summer the central highlands and the north coast probably offer walkers the best options.

Choosing the best month for tourists to visit the island is not easy. Even during the 'rainy season', Madeiran deep winter is certain to be better than anywhere in northern Europe. Generally speaking, the island is most popular among older people who wish to avoid major temperature fluctuations for health reasons. For those seeking rest or recuperation, the 'blossom months' (March to May and August to October) are probably the best. For the more active tourist keen on hill walking or swimming, then high summer is recommended. For golfers and tennis enthusiasts, any of the summer months from April to September would be suitable.

Madeira should, however, not be regarded as a beach resort; many people use the swimming pools — usually heated and sometimes with sea water — in most larger hotels.

Do not be tempted to leave your warm pullover at home. In the higher regions and in the evenings in the coastal areas, the weather can turn quite cool.

Fauna and Flora

Madeira enjoys a favourable climate and particularly in spring and autumn, visitors to the island will discover a blaze of colour.

For those visitors who wish to extend their knowledge of Madeira's flora, Funchal tourist office and local bookshops sell multilingual, illustrated guides to the island's plants and flowers.

Just take a look around: bougainvillea in all their colours, freesias, geraniums, bright red poinsettias, jasmine, amaryllis, lilies, olive green aloes, gladioli, begonia, chrysanthemum, antirrhinums and marigolds, hyacinths, violets, magnolia, camellia and the finest orchids, probably the best known of which belong to the spring-flowering cymbidium family. High summer sees the anthurium in flower, while in deep winter the lady's slipper orchid is the highlight.

Despite their short lives, flowers from Madeira, the flower island, make excellent presents. Many of the tender orchids which thrive here travel well. Dip the stalks in lukewarm water for a few hours when you get home and they will quickly regain their fresh appearance. Sadly, they are only available from February to May. On the other hand, the bird-of paradise flowers (strelitzia) bloom through-

Bananas are an important crop, especially near the south coast

Hibiscus adds a bright splash of colour throughout Madeira

MADEIRA IN BLOOM

Many people visit Madeira to see the tropical flowers that the island is so well-known for. Some are native to the island, but many are cultivated, and some grow so profusely that you would think that they are wild plants. Others, which are grown as small house plants in northern Europe, grow outside as large shrubs or bushes. Although many flower all-year-round and others have overlapping seasons, the following selected list is a good general guide to when plants may be seen at their best.

All-Year-Round
African hemp
Angel's trumpet
Begonia
Bourgainvillea
Brazilian spider plant
Flamingo
Plumbago
Popcorn bush
Strelitzia (bird of
    Paradise)

Spring Flowering
Caffre bean tree
Cape chestnut
Cat's claw vine
Cock's comb coral
    tree
Flame tree
Indian shot
Judas tree
King protea
Madeira holly
Mexican orange
    flower
Painted trumpet
Parrot's bill
Passion flower

Red passion flower
Red Valerian
Spear lily
Stiff bottlebush

Summer Flowering
African tulip
Agapanthus
Century plant
Everlasting
Garden coral
Love's chain
Madonna lily
Mealy stonecrop
Mexican blood
    trumpet
Noble kaffir lily
Nolina
Pagoda tree
Red hot poker
Silk tree

Autumn Flowering
Belladonna lily
Dragon tree
Canary creeper
Chinese hat plant
Guernsey lily

Kapok tree
Madeira Goodyera
Mexican blue palm
Red flowering gum

Winter Flowering
California geranium
Calla lily
Camel's foot
Cattleya
Climbing aloe
Coral tree
Cumbidium
Flame tree
Golden shower
Japanese rubber plant
Kaffir lily
Kaffir tree
Lady slipper
Maguey plant
Mimosa
Peruvian magic tree
Poisettia
Red hot poker
Sword aloe
Winter weeping
    bottlebrush

out the year and their strong growth makes them perhaps better suited to long journeys. Those people who grow their own plants and flowers, should ask in the botanical gardens about cuttings.

In spring the delicate lilac flowers of the jacaranda tree adorn Funchal's main roads, as the blooms emerge from the leaves. At higher altitudes the splendour of acacia dominates and some of the mountain roads are lined with hydrangea. Madeira viper's bugloss (Pride of Madeira) with its first reddish, then blue flowers is frequently to be seen growing alongside footpaths and *levadas*.

Memories will linger of the changing vegetation on the mountain sides. Sub-tropical flowers resplendent at lower levels are followed at higher altitudes by weather-beaten tree heaths and small alpines.

In the north of the island, many of the original dense laurel woods can still be seen, although interspersed here and there are junipers together with tree ferns, tree heaths, chestnuts and cedars up to 30m (100ft) in height. On the south side of the island the woodlands are less dense due to the lower rainfall levels and, in many places, forest has given way to agricultural land. Oak, spruce, larch, beech and parasol pine flourish as well as one or two dragon trees. Eucalyptus and maritime pine have also been planted. In the island's parks and botanical gardens, unusual species include the red sandalwood, Australian acacias and the African sausage tree.

Fruit are plentiful with strawberries ripening from March to August. Cherries and apricots are available in May and June, pawpaws and figs from June to October, melons from August to October, mango and avocado pears from September to December, apples and pears from October to March, grapefruit and oranges from November to January and bananas all the year round.

Early vegetables and cereals are grown exclusively for consumption on the island and sugar cane just for local rum production. Flowers, pineapples, fruit, pulses, sweet potatoes, onions and, of course, wine are exported. Visitors are sure to see attractive leafy walkways created from vines which have been allowed to reach head height before being secured to frames. In some places the vines are grown up trellises like fruit. Given Madeira's favourable climate, this important crop will thrive anywhere below 800m (2,625ft) above sea-level. The grape harvest takes place in August and September.

Madeira's fauna includes 200 bird species, mainly migratory, only thirty-five of which breed on the island. The only bird exclusive to the island is the Madeira wood pigeon. Countless types of butterflies will be seen, as well as lizards and harmless insects, mosquitoes in summer and also bats. 'Imported' animals, many of which are hunted, include pigeons, partridges, quails and rabbits. Semi-wild mountain goats roam freely on the higher slopes and trout fishing is popular in mountain streams.

The cattle, which have also had to be brought over from mainland Europe, have very little grazing land and the farmers keep their stock in cowsheds known as *palheiros*. Inside these thatched huts, the animals are fed and milked, singly or in pairs and Madeiran cows are

The evil-looking espada, *or scabbard fish, with razor-sharp teeth is a delicious Madeiran speciality to be found on most menus*

in fact noted for their creamy milk. Beef and dairy products are also exported.

Fish and shellfish are found in abundance around the shores of Madeira and over 100 species are fished including cod, swordfish, redfish, pollack, squid, tuna, mackerel and barracuda. Again, many of these are exported either raw or processed. The *espada* (scabbard or cutlass fish) lives at great depths, as indicated by its great staring eyes designed to make use of the very small amount of light that reaches them. They are only found in the waters around Madeira and near Japan — they can only survive in the depths and are usually dead by the time the fishing lines are hauled to the surface. Most *espadas* are caught by the fishermen from Câmara de Lobos.

A 200,000sq km (77,000sq miles) area of sea surrounding the archipelago has been designated as the National Sea Mammal Park. It is intended to offer protection to the numerous species of whale and dolphin as well as the endangered monk seal. This primitive aquatic mammal can still be found in the Desertas — the deserted islands — where the many sea-washed caves serve both as sleeping quarters and nurseries. Several of the one-time whale catchers of Madeira now act as the policemen of the seas. The headquarters of this new environmental protection agency has been opened at the whaling museum in Caniçal.

No sharks are found in the Madeiran archipelago.

Locally grown fruit and vegetables are sold in the market at Funchal

The People

While the Canary Islands have been inhabited for thousands of years, Madeira was first settled in 1419. A lot of backbreaking work was required, first to clear the forests and then to build the terraces and create viable agricultural land. These first settlers were Portuguese, some from aristocratic families. Despite Italian, Moorish and African influences and Spanish and English rule, Portuguese language, customs and traditions still predominate — 900km (560miles) from the mainland and under 600km (370miles) west of Morocco. Madeirans look back proudly at their ancestry with roots established well over 500 years ago.

The island's total population exceeds 290,000, but most live on the sheltered southern coast. The capital, Funchal, the island's economic and tourist centre, is where a good third of Madeirans live and work. Many of the population are employed on the land, as fishermen or in the food processing industry. Service trades and tourism also provide considerable employment opportunities. The generous hospitality of the islanders, Madeira's natural beauty and its pleasant climate combine to create an enchanting holiday destination.

On arrival, many visitors will be struck by the unusual clothing worn by some of the islanders. For example, at Monte look out for the 'sledge-drivers' with their white trousers, white shirt and 'boater' or the women from the country areas dressed in black. Their menfolk — particularly in the rural uplands — would not dream of setting foot outside without their brown, woollen caps, ear flaps pulled up or down depending on the weather. The flower sellers of Funchal are also often traditionally dressed in brightly-coloured costumes with white blouses, red bodices, capes and striped coats — and on their heads, not just the flower baskets, but a small black cap known as a *carapuça*, the 'lightning conductor' with red trimmings and a long stalk. Both men and women wear boots of yellow calfskin.

Traditional costumes are more in evidence in the south-west of the island and even then, only appear for the festivals mostly during the summer months. The majority of the population is Roman Catholic and in the smaller communities many of these festivities are conducted in traditional style. One small local festival is known as *Arraial*, while another island-wide celebration is for the *romarias* who travel across the island in a kind of pilgrimage. The fun really starts on the day before with boisterous celebrations, singing, dancing, rockets, fire-wheels rolling down the hillsides and bonfires blazing at the top. *Espetadas* and wine make the perfect combination. The following morning a procession winds through the town.

Apart from the New Year celebrations which start in Funchal on 30 December and continue until New Year's Day and the high-spirited festivities on the two Thursdays before the Brazilian-style Carnival in February, other important festivals include the celebrations for São João and São Pedro in June. However, Madeira's biggest celebrations in honour of Nossa Senhora do Monte, Madeira's patron saint, take place in Monte on 14 and 15 August. The festival of São Pedro, the patron saint of fishermen, is an important occasion in Santa Cruz, Camara de Lobos and Ribeira Brava, while in September in Ponta Delgada, 'Men's Day' is celebrated. On 9 October, Machico holds the Festival of the Miracles of Christ with a procession. Given the number of *festas* both large and small, which are well spaced out throughout the year, it ought to be possible for every visitor to witness at least one of these religious festivals.

April and May is the time of year for the flower festivals with one important three-day celebration taking place in Funchal towards the end of April. Competitions cover the various types of decorations and there is always a colourful procession. In June many villages hold a sheep shearing festival, a task which is usually undertaken by women! Tourists are always welcomed as spectators. September is wine festival time and again visitors are invited to join in the wine tasting and dancing.

The bigger hotels provide entertainments which usually include folk dancing by one of the many local dancing groups. Traditional music and dancing invariably go together.

Madeira's four-stringed guitar is known as a *braguinha* and percussion accompaniment is provided by a *brinquinho*. Dolls slide up and down a pole and castanets and bells on the dolls' backs maintain the beat. The *bailinho* leads the dancing.

Three main dances can usually be identified and interpreted by the spectator. Two refer to working on the land — carrying heavy baskets and treading the grapes — the third originated in Ponta do Sol, the home of many of the black slaves brought over from Africa to work on the sugar plantations. In this dance, the dancers move in a circle taking short steps with their heads bowed in the manner of chained slaves. The rhythm of the music has a distinct African flavour.

As well as the casino, three international events draw tourists to Madeira every year. Funchal's music festival is organised in June, for two days in August a motor rally takes over the island's coast road and a bridge tournament is held every June in Funchal.

The island is well known for its handicrafts with Madeiran embroidery, basket-making, pottery and inlaid wooden items recognised in Europe and beyond. These crafts go back to the times when a spare time occupation was necessary if working outdoors was out of the question or there was nothing left to do in the kitchen. Hence these specialised skills flourished within the home or as small cottage industries.

Embroidery and tapestry-making are the best known and the work for these items is generally undertaken at home although the basic designs are factory produced. Visitors to the island who wish to do more than watch grandmother at work can go back to school. Embroidery schools have been established in Machico and Camara

The traditional way of life still carries on in the western part of Madeira

de Lobos and they are open to visitors. Experts will explain the differences between traditional *richelieu* and *cavaca* or newer *appliqué* and shadow embroidery methods. In order that quality and prices are guaranteed, the Madeiran Institute of Embroidery, Tapestry and Handicrafts checks the products and awards a special seal.

The commercial development of home embroidery dates from the middle of the nineteenth century when Miss Phelps, an English resident, presented her friends with small samples of the local women's work. Initially British and also German companies placed firm orders, but still only six of the ninety-seven companies are in foreign hands. They provide work for about 70,000 women, making table cloths, serviettes, handkerchiefs and embroidered fabric for blouses etc.

Tapestry making on a commercial basis was introduced as recently as 1938 when the German artist, Herbert Kiekeben, on the look-out for new ways to express the island's beauty, painted pictures on to canvas which were then sewn. Although the main motifs are floral, other tapestries are reproductions of old masters and not just local landscapes or Madeiran themes. The wall hangings, cushion covers, upholstery, handbags and 'paintings' use over 2,500 colour shades.

The rather coarse cloth and linen woven by Madeiran peasant farmers from wool and thread is of a better quality than normal household fabric. This is the island's oldest cottage industry and one usually borne of necessity. Homespun wool was used to make the cloth for trousers and flax was used for shirts, coats, towels, bed linen and tablecloths. When purchasing any of these items, check that they carry a 'Made in Madeira' label.

Madeira's basketry and wicker industry also has its roots among the rural poor, particularly the men, who made baskets when winter or bad weather prevented them from working on the land or going to sea. Supple willow shoots are readily available and provide the ideal material for baskets and cane furniture. The willow is cut, peeled and then dried in the sun. To make sure that the cane can be worked easily, it must be boiled for a few hours before use.

About 150 years ago commercial production started up in the village of Camacha some 12km (7miles) from Funchal. Now 70 per cent of all the island's wicker products are made here. Over 1,000 different articles are manufactured ranging from simple shopping baskets to elaborate garden furniture with retractable foot stools. The quality of such products is demonstrated by the total absence of any nail, wire or adhesive.

The wicker industry is still looking for new products and the latest additions to the range include baskets and bags woven from the fibrous bark of the banana palm.

The visitor to Madeira will certainly find plenty of other handmade crafts on display and one of them is bound to make a perfect souvenir. A cassette of Madeiran folk music would provide the right atmosphere should you wish to re-create a memorable Madeiran meal to accompany the bottle of madeira you bought. Remember, however, that there are restrictions to the quantity of wine, madeira or otherwise, you are able to take home with you.

Food and Drink

Madeira's menus offer many dishes which visitors to the island are sure to be familiar with but they also include many tasty surprises. Of course local produce plays a vital part in the Madeiran diet with a tremendous range of fish and seafood on offer, but examples of international and traditional European dishes can also be found on most menus.

Lunch is eaten between 12.30 and 2.30pm and the evening meal is usually served around 7pm. Generally speaking a fish (or egg) dish follows the hors d'oeuvre and then a meat dish with vegetables precedes the dessert or fruit.

One Madeiran delicacy that should be tried is the black scabbard fish or *espada* — not to be confused with *espadarte* (swordfish) or *espetada* (skewered beef). After the black skin has been scraped off it is fried in olive oil, or it may also be boiled or steamed and is usually served with lots of onions, tomatoes or cheese. In some recipes, garlic, herbs and white wine are often added. Tuna (*atum*) fish fillets are another local speciality. *Caldeirada* is a fish soup based on a simple recipe but with many variations.

Carne de vinhos e alhos is another local dish in which salted fatty pork, bay leaves and garlic are marinated in wine and then fried in pork dripping.

Espetadas are a type of kebab in which chunks of meat are spit-roasted over a charcoal fire. They are usually saved for festivals, when they are eaten with *Bolo de caco*. This is a type of bread — literally translated it means 'bread slice' — in which a well-kneaded dough of flour, sweet potatoes, salt, pepper and water are baked on an extremely hot stone or between clay tiles.

Party snacks are not served on bread or crackers but often on *Milho cozido*, cold cornmeal biscuits in which thin wafers of the thick dough are fried in olive oil until crispy and then topped with pieces of cheese or an olive. In country areas, fried cornmeal is often served

MADEIRA WINE

The unique character of Madeira is in part due to the *estufagem* or special heating process which is unique to this fortified wine. After the harvest the wine is stored in casks in special lodges (*estufa*) at 45 °C (112 °F) for a minimum of three months. The wine is gradually cooled and then begins a normal maturing period.

All Madeiras are blends, except vintages which are made from the finest wines, exclusively from a traditional grape variety, and are matured for a minimum of twenty years in the cask and a further two years in the bottle.

The special Madeira process was discovered in the eighteenth century when it was noticed that shipments to the tropics not only survived the stifling heat, but also aquired attractive qualities and incredible longevity. The finest Madeiras can remain in excellent condition for 150 years or more! Madeira wine was even used as ballast in ships bound for the West and East Indies with the sole purpose of subjecting them to as much equatorial heat as possible.

There are four main varieties, each named after the grape from which it is made:

Sercial — dry, smooth and light-bodied, it is ideally served chilled as an aperitif. The vine for Sercial is the Riesling from the Rhine.

Verdelho — medium dry, light and elegant with a tangy, fine-texture. It may be drunk as a table wine and has become very popular.

Malmsey — also known as **Malvasia** — is dark, full-bodied and sweet. Generally reckoned to be the finest madeira wine, its vines come from the south-eastern tip of the Peloponnese peninsula.

Bual — full bodied and fruity with a well rounded flavour and attractive smoky complexity. The vines come from Burgundy.

Malmsey and Bual are both dessert wines.

---

warm with a sauce made from tomato and onion or pieces of mackerel or dried cod. Air-dried cod or *bacalhau* plays an important part in Portuguese cuisine.

At Christmas, *Bolo de mel* or honey cakes and candied fruit are favourite desserts. They are often bought as gifts when visiting family and friends.

Many drinks are made from the island's wide range of fruit. Lemonade is popular as is a liquor made from passion fruit, which was introduced from Brazil. *Maracuja*, the Brazilian word for this fruit, has been retained. Lemon juice flavoured with honey and rum or *poncha* is another refreshing drink.

Madeira wine is of course the island's most famous drink. Often fortified with brandy, not all madeira is suitable as a table wine. The wine is heated, sometimes for several months and consequently it is a durable wine which will keep for years, even if opened. Many Madeiran wine cellars allow tasting.

In the rural communities, the favourite wine is a light red which is produced in the north of the island, while *Aguardente*, a spirit made from sugar cane and grapes, is also very popular. The locally brewed Coral beer is recommended.

Getting Around Madeira

This book describes tours of the island from the capital, Funchal. Transport is assumed to be by hired car, but scheduled bus services could also be used instead. The tourist information office can provide timetables. If there are several people in your party, then a taxi is the best alternative. If you wish to spend a large part of the day on one activity, sunbathing on the beach at Prainha or walking, then ask the driver to take you there and arrange to be picked up at the same spot or some other agreed meeting-place (pay the fare on the return journey).

To enjoy the tours to the full and to spend some time walking along the *levadas* it may be necessary to booking overnight accommodation in hotels outside the main tourist centres of Funchal, Caniço and Machico. Plan carefully before undertaking any such trip by car and remember that driving on the mainly narrow and winding mountain roads on the island is not an easy task. The driver will need to concentrate and so may missing much of the island's charm and beauty. These tours use the more interesting older roads, but a new motorway will eventually link the airport and Funchal with Ribeira Brava which will make short trips from the capital to the west of the island more practical and less of an exausting expedition.

The following tours of Madeira are broken into sections so that the visitors can prepare their own itinerary, while the last part of the book has forty walks of various grades of difficulty, ranging from easy *levada* walks to mountain excursions which should only be undertaken by experienced walkers.

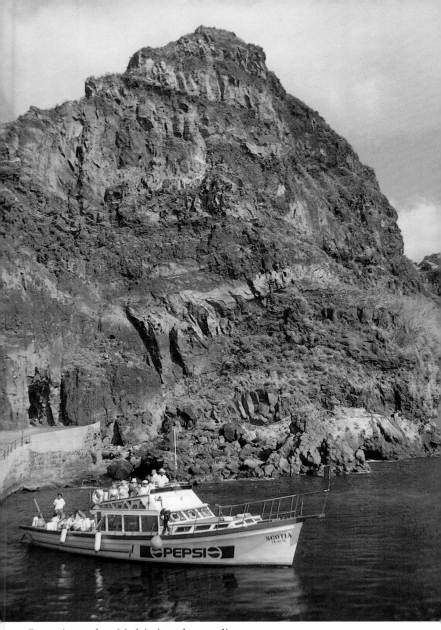

Boat trips explore Madeira's rocky coastline

1
FUNCHAL

Funchal means 'wild fennel place' after the medicinal plant which the first settlers found growing in abundance here. Today the city has a population of around 100,000 and is by far the biggest place on the island. It is the administrative centre of the Portuguese Funchal district which comprises the whole of the Madeiran archipelago. It offered the first settlers only a small beach at the mouth of three small rivers, but it was the biggest they could find. Situated on the south coast, it occupied a sheltered position and was soon to grow into the island's principal settlement. It enjoyed town status as early as 1508.

The streets and houses of Funchal extend inland up the hills like the rows and aisles of an open-air theatre with the vast Atlantic Ocean as the stage. The narrow streets of the old town nestle against the shore line as if they are the theatre's orchestra pit. These streets, a symphony of colour, have witnessed 500 years of history, but there is no denying the discord created by the arrival in Funchal of the twentieth century.

In February many of the main streets are alive with the lilac flowers of the jacaranda tree and orange bignonias clamber up the walls of the brightly washed houses. Multi-coloured bougainvillea attached to netting spreads over the tiled roofs. It is also used to camouflage Funchal's less attractive rivers. These three rivers run in deep gorges through the centre of the city and in normal conditions they are no more than a trickle — it is only after heavy rain that the need for such deep water channels is appreciated. In October 1993 the worst storm for a century caused all three rivers to overflow, leaving five dead, hundreds homeless and a trail of destruction.

The busy dual-carriageway Avenida das Comunidades Madeirenses (formerly called Avenida do Mar and still shown as such on many maps) runs alongside the sea front. From the western end a jetty linking Loo and Pontinha Rock protects the harbour and bay. Now it is where the luxury cruise liners come alongside, while in earlier days they anchored outside the harbour and their passengers came ashore in smaller vessels.

For a long time, Madeira has been a popular port of call for cruise ships on route to distant destinations. The aeroplane is displacing the liner, but Funchal is nevertheless still a favourite stopover for ocean-going sailors. Faster forms of transport have of course brought with them high-speed tourists and there are already many places in the town where mass tourism has left its mark. Despite its remoteness, Funchal has not been able to ignore the demands of modern tourists. It is no longer a sleepy backwater, yet there is still much of charm for those who can ignore the bustle and traffic snarl-ups of the central area. Sunday is generally much quieter.

Saunter through the streets and narrow alleys, climb the steep inclines and meander down again, past the silent statues and the splashing fountains. Cross the shady squares and pass in front of the houses which tell a story of more peaceful times. Many of the street names alone have their own tales to tell.

Look out for Rua do Infançia (Street of Childhood), Rua do Difficuldades (Street of Difficulties), Rua do Mãe dos Homens (Street of the Mother of Man) or Rua dos Arrependidos (Street of the Penitent). You can stroll down Travessa do Descanso (Alley of Repose), investigate Travessa da Saudade (Wistful Alley), Travessa do Frigorifico (Refrigerator Alley), Beco do Pão Duro (Dry Bread Lane), Largo do Foguete (Honey Water Way), Travessa da Conveniencia (Comfort Lane) and Azinhaga dos Ausentes (Absentees' Cutting).

Allow yourself to be captivated by the atmosphere of a place where old-fashioned charm stands in sullen opposition to stifling modernity, a place situated between mountains and oceans where the sea mist smells of traffic fumes — where the old world meets the new.

Central Funchal (West)

Like most cities there is traffic congestion, a one-way system and parking is very difficult, so visit the centre of Funchal on foot, or use the town's bus service or a taxi if you just want to visit one or two of the outying places. At the **Tourist Information Office**, a booklet is available with details of bus access to the main tourist sights in and around Funchal and on the rest of the island. There is no bus station as such, but most leave from the eastern end of the promenade, some from Rua Brigadeiro Oudinot near the market, others from near the

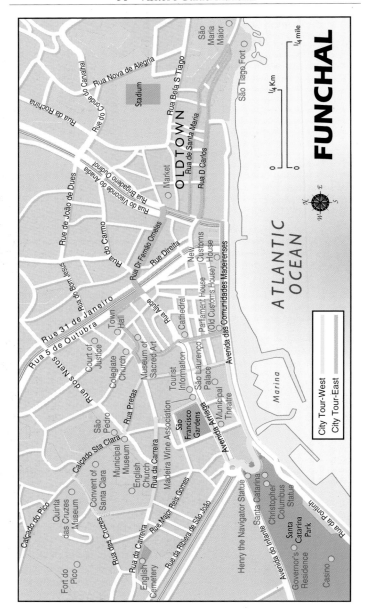

FUNCHAL

ATLANTIC OCEAN

OLDTOWN

São Tiago Fort

São Maria Maior

Rua Bela S.Tiago

Rua Nova de Alegria

Rua do Conde do Carvalhal

Rua da Rochinha

Rua do Conde

Stadium

Rua de Santa Maria

Rua D Carlos

Market

Rua do Visconde do Anadia

Rua Brigadeiro Oudinot

Rua de João de Dues

Rua do Carmo

Rua Dr Fernão Ornelas

Rua Direita

New Customs House

Parliament House (Old Customs House)

Avenida das Comunidades Madeirenses

Cathedral

Rua Aljube

Rua 31 de Janeiro

Rua das Bom Jesus

Rua 5 de Outubra

Rua dos Netos

Town Hall

Court of Justice

Collegiate Church

Museum of Sacred Art

Tourist Information

São Lourenço Palace

São Pedro

Rua Pretas

Calçado Sta Clara

Municipal Museum

Municipal Theatre

Avenida Arriaga

São Francisco Gardens

Madeira Wine Association

Rua da Carreira

English Church

Convent of Santa Clara

Quinta das Cruzes Museum

Calçado do Pico

Rua das Cruzes

Rua Major Reis Gomes

Rua da Carreira

Rua da Ribeira de São João

Fort do Pico

English Cemetery

Henry the Navigator Statue

Santa Catarina

Christopher Columbus Statue

Santa Catarina Park

Avenida do Infante

Governor's Residence

Casino

Rua da Pontinho

Marina

City Tour-West

City Tour-East

N W E S

0 ¼ Km

0 ¼ mile

São Lourenço Fortress, now houses the Regional Government of Madeira

Funchal and the Fort do Pico from the Hotel São João

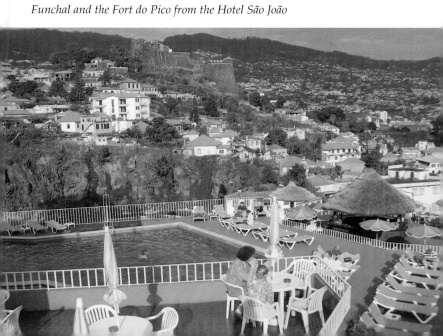

main Post Office on Rua da Ribeira de San João. Hotel receptionists will provide information on the nearest bus stop. Taking a taxi is another possibility. The numbers in brackets refer to the town plan.

As it would take too long to do justice to the city in one tour, the suggested walks round central Funchal are divided into west and east of Avenida Zarco.

As most of the tourist hotels are to the west of the centre, a logical place to start is in **Parque de Sante Catarina**. In the park is the **Capela de Santa Catarina**, erected in the seventeenth century on the instructions of the wife of João Gonçalves Zarco on the site of Madeira's first chapel. A statue of Christopher Columbus stands nearby, commemorating his short stay in Funchal, as well as the well-known modern sculpture *The Sower*, which originally stood in the city centre. At the top end of the park, near the pink and white Quinta Vigia, where the president of Madeiria's regional government lives, is a preserved steam roller that came from England and an old wine-making machine.

From the park there is a good view down on to the harbour where the cruise ships berth, and the seventeenth-century 23m (75ft) high **Loo Rock fortress**. It occupies a central position on the breakwater and is still used by the military. Its fourteen cannons are still used to welcome in the New Year. On the breakwater and a little nearer to the shore lies a smaller rock known as the Pontinha Rock. It too was fortified in earlier times.

Leave the park, passing the monument to **Henry the Navigator**, the man largely responsible for projecting Portugal on to the world stage, on the Praça do Infante at the end of Avenida Arriaga. Walk along Avenida das Comunidades Madeirenses (Avenida do Mar) to the **São Lourenço Fortress**. It has been altered many times, but is now houses the Regional Government of Madeira. The tower dates from the sixteenth century as Manuel II's well maintained coat-of-arms demonstrates. The walls of the fortress date from the seventeenth century. Above the entrance door on the corner beside a small square is a portrait of St Laurence. On the port side of the building, an old well is still visible. In earlier times Funchal's townsfolk collected their water from here. The fort is not open to the public, but there is a small military museum on the northern side.

Opposite the fort is the marina and a sailing yacht, once owned by the Beatles, which is now permanently moored as a floaing restaurant. Turn left up the side of the fort along Avenida Zarco, to the **statue of João Gonçalves Zarco**, the discoverer of Madeira, which stands in the centre of the town at the junction of Avenida de Arriaga and Avenida de Zarco, close to the Government Offices.

Continue up Avenida Zarco, then up Rua Pretas (take care as it is a narrow one-way street busy with traffic) to the **Museu Municipal** at 35 Rua Mouraria. This was formerly Palacio do São Pedro, a count's palace dating from the eighteenth century, but it now houses a collection of fish and birds to be found in and around Madeira. Most of the exhibits are stuffed, although sixty live fish can be seen in the adjoining aquarium. The museum also houses a completely different type of exhibit, the Sword of João Gonçalves Zarco, the man responsible for the discovery of Madeira. He was a man of humble origins but fell in love with a noblewoman. Just as in the fairy tales, he sought fame and honour in order to marry her and he succeeded. He showed great courage in several battles and became a knight.

The building also houses the Archives of Madeira and the Municipal Library. Opposite is the church of **São Pedro** (St Peter).

Further up the road is the former **Santa Clara convent**; entry is through a rather unprepossessing door. The church contains the tombs of the Zarco family, the grand tomb canopied tomb of João Gonçalves is particularly striking. An ornate Moorish ceiling is well maintained as is a floor of green tiles. The wall with *azulejos* dates from the beginning of the seventeenth century and the seats in the lower porch are eighteenth century. It is probably the most decorative church on the island. The monastery is now used as a mission school for the Franciscan Order. It was first built in the fifteenth century and renovated 200 years later. Zarco's granddaughter is said to have been the convent's founder. Orange trees grow in the courtyard of the impressive cloister.

Climb still further up the hill to reach the interesting **Museu da** **Quinta das Cruzes**, Madeira's museum for the decorative arts, situated just above the Santa Clara convent, at 1 Calçada do Pico. The villa which houses the collection has been restored and is thought that João Gonçalves Zarco lived in the original building (of which two Manueline doorways survive) prior to his death. Other parts date from 1692, but the main building was enlarged after partial destruction of the house after an earthquake in 1748. The many rooms of the museum are furnished in the style of the period. Also on display is some fine porcelain, Portuguese and English antique furniture as well rare cupboards made from the wood used for transporting sugar. The 'Archaeological Garden' contains two stone window surrounds in Manueline style and over fifty stone carvings from demolished houses. The flower garden is another example of the well-tended parks that lovers of flora should include in their itinerary of Funchal. There are also some superb orchids.

Another fort, the **Fortaleza do Pico**, stands higher up the mountain

Statue of João Gonçalves Zarco, the discoverer of Madeira

The cathedral, hemmed in by Funchal's heavy traffic

slopes above the museum. It was built during the Spanish occupation around 1600, but now accommodates a marine radio station. The fort seems to dominate Funchal and is best seen from afar.

Return to the centre down Rua das Cruzes, just below the museum. Just a short distance along here is a breathtaking panoramic view over the town and port. Beneath stands the domed **English church**. It was built in 1822 along the lines of the Pantheon in Rome, as a law prohibited the construction of non-Catholic churches in the style of a Christian church. It is part of the Diocese of Gibraltar. Until 1770, when a British cemetery was laid out, all Protestants who died in Madeira had to be buried at sea.

Drop down onto Rua da Carreira and turn left. This street is full of interesting old buildings with decorative cast-iron balconies, although many are now but a faded glory of their former splendour. Turn right down the narrow Rua São Francisco to the small **Jardim do São Francisco** with exotic trees, colourful gardens and an ornamental pond with black swans. The gardens are on the site of a Franciscan monastery; on the western side is the Scottish Kirk, founded in 1895

You are now back on the busy Avenida Arriaga. A short way along to the left is the **São Francisco Wine Lodge**, operated by the Madeira Wine Association, which includes most of the famous names of the Madeira wine trade. This is the oldest working wine lodge in Funchal, in a building which was, from the sixteenth century, part of the Franciscan Monastery. There are tours, an audio-visual show about Maderia wine, a working cooperage, a wine museum, tastings, and of course an opportunity to buy the various types, including some of the finest and rarest vintages. It is an interesting way of spending an hour or so, especially if the weather is poor. Further along is the **Tourist Information Office**, where town plans are available and other leaflets give tourists details on such things as opening times, bus routes and schedules.

Opposite the Jardim do São Francisco is the former Chamber of Commerce, now a car showroom, decorated with painted tiles showing, in a rather romanticised manner, scenes from traditional Madeiran life. Next door is the **Municipal Theatre** built in the 1880s and recently completely restored to its original glory.

Central Funchal (East)

This tour of the eastern part of the city centre starts on the sea front promenade, one block east of the São Laurenço fort. Here is the **Alfandega Velha** or Old Customs House, now used to house the

Madeiran Parliament. Dating originally from the fifteenth century, it was extended in the eighteenth century but many features of Manueline architecture were retained. Of particular interest are the portals and windows, as are the two marvellous Moorish-style ceilings and vaulting supported by figured capitals on the ground floor. The modern circular debating chamber, while satisfactory as a modern structure, seems incongruous when tacked onto the front of the old building.

Walk up Rua João Tavira to Funchal's **cathedral** or Sé, which stands at the top of the Avenida de Arriaga. Its 46m (150ft) high tower with its colourful tiled spire has become a symbol for the town. Built between 1485 and 1514 out of local black and red stone, it is partly painted white and from the outside is simple and dignified. Commissioned by the Order of Christ, at the time of its construction it was Portugal's first overseas bishopric. The portal is a fine example of Madeiran Manueline architecture.

Inside the cluttered interior, the magnificently carved choir stall and the cedarwood ceiling are the most striking, although the ceiling is not easy to see in the gloom. Inlaid ivory in the woodwork reflects the contemporary style of Manuel II and exemplifies his influence. A painting from the Flemish school adorns the high altar, while one of the adjoining altars is dedicated to the much revered Virgin of Fatima. The small town north of Lisbon where the Virgin Mary appeared before a young girl has become a 'Portuguese Lourdes'.

It was near the cathedral that Madeira's first sugar plantation was located and Funchal's coat-of-arms still bears five sugar cones.

Continue up Rua João Tavira and turn right at the top to the Praça do Município. Before visiting the square you might like to turn left to see the **Vicente Photographic Museum** in an interesting old building with iron balconies round a courtyard. This was Madeira's first photographic studio, set up in 1865, which amassed over half a million negatives of Maderian life. The town hall square has a decorative back and white mosaic patterned pavement with a central fountain. On the north side stand the imposing **Ingreja do Colégio** (Collegiate Church) and the adjoining former Jesuit college; they were built in the seventeenth century on the site of the Franciscans' first monastery. The college was once used to billet British troops, and is now part of Funchal University. Behind the palatial façade of the church, with four marble statues of saints, stand the main chapel and side chapel both decorated in a rich baroque style. The colourful frieze on the sacristy wall, made with *azulejos* in traditional Portuguese style, is particularly interesting, as are the *azulejos* on the floor of the main nave.

On the south side of the square in the former bishop's palace, entrance in Rua do Bispo, is the **Museu de Arte Sacra**, the Museum of Sacred Art. Built in 1750, the building now accommodates treasures from some of the island's old churches as well as sculptures, ecclesiastical robes and paintings, many of fifteenth-century Flemish origin which are believed to have arrived in Madeira in exchange for sugar. A nativity scene with the three kings, once displayed behind the altar in the church at Machico, is perhaps the most impressive of the works on display, although Memling's St James and the portrayal of dragon-slayer St George as a baby are also of interest.

The **town hall**, built in the style typical of the late eighteenth century, was once the private residence of one of Madeira's wealthiest landowners. Take a look at the inner patio with its fountain and decorative *azulejos*. Upstairs is the small, and free, **Museu da Cidade** (City Museum), with early paintings and prints of Funchal, models, old photographs and artifacts showing the history of the city.

Go along the right-hand side of the town hall, turn right and then cross the Ribeira de Santa Luzia. Walk down Rua Dr Fernão Ornelas, a busy shopping steet and cross the Ribeira de João Gomes to the **Mercado dos Lavradores** or Workers' Market Hall. This dates from 1941 and is a hive of activity with much local produce on sale. Here there are two floors selling locally grown fruit, vegetables, flowers and groceries, while the fish hall sells *espada* (scabbard fish), tuna and other locally caught varieties.

Further east the **old fishing quarter** extends up into the town along narrow alleys. The area is now more popular with artists than fisherfolk, but the early morning **fish market** is always popular with both buyers and sightseers and the district's many fish restaurants and less salubrious bars stay open until the early hours.

Near the old town is the seventeenth-century **São Tiago Fort** (now used for exhibitions and summer concerts) and the later **Santa Maria Maior church**, with a striking whitewashed baroque façade. Every May Day is a festival in honour of James, the younger apostle who is thought to have protected the fishermen from two serious epidemics in the sixteenth century.

From the market you can return along Avenida das Comunidades Madeirenses, passing the New Customs House, or cross the two river bridges and wander through the narrow shopping streets which lie between the Parliament Building and the cathedral.

Out from the centre of Funchal are some other churches of interest. These include **Igreja da Encarnaçao** which is situated to the north of the town centre. Exhibiting features of the Manueline style, it dates from the fifteenth and sixteenth centuries. The chapel in the **Nazaré**

Funchal's flower sellers dress in traditional costume

All manner of local produce is for sale at the 'Workers' Market' in Funchal

district of the town also contains some interesting eighteenth-century *azulejos*. It lies above the town to the west and offers a fine view over Funchal bay.

The **Igreja de Boa Nova** is a modern church on the north-eastern edge of the town beside the road to Camacha, but parts of the previous baroque structure have been skilfully incorporated into its structure. Here too a viewing terrace provides visitors with a view over Funchal.

Funchal — West of the Centre

Most of Funchal's tourist hotel development has been west of the centre beyond the Parque de Sante Catarina, along Estrada Monumental. This has prevented the centre of the city from being over-developed with high-rise buildings.

Just a little further out from the park is the **Casino** which form part of an extraordinary complex of buildings, including a luxury hotel and congress centre. It was designed by Oscar Niemeyer, the famous architect responsible for Brasilia, Brazil's ultra-modern capital. The casino also contains a wide selection of slot machines, the notorious 'one-armed bandits', so that visitors to the town who have not brought their evening dress can still enjoy the thrill of playing games of chance.

Most of Funchal's modern hotels are to the west of the city, near the Lido

✳ Behind the Hotel Quinta do Sol, on Rua do Dr Pita, the road going up to the Barreiros football stadium, is the **Quinta Magnolia Sports Centre**. This is the former British Country Club, set in gardens, where facilities included tennis (floodlit), squash, jogging track and swimmming pool; reservation is usually recommended.

🏛 Estrada Monumental passes **Reid's Hotel**, one of the world's great hotels, standing in its own gardens on a headland with fantastic views. Founded over a century ago by Scotsman William Reid, many famous people have stayed here, from George Bernard Shaw to Sir Winston Churchill and Gregory Peck. (Walk 1 to the Soccoridos valley and Câmara de Lobos starts from here.)

✳ Further west is the Lido, where due to Madeira's shortage of beaches, a large swimming pool complex has been built into the rocks. Most hotels, of course, have their own pools.

Additional Information

Places to Visit

Exposição Permanente
Fortaleza São Lourenço
Avenida Zarco

Mercado dos Lavradores (market)
Rua Profetas
Open: Monday 7am-2pm, Tuesday-Thursday 7am-4pm, Friday 6am-8pm, Saturday 6am-4pm

Museu da Cidade
Nos Paços do Concelho do Funchal
Open: Monday-Friday 9am-12.30pm. 2-5pm

Museu da Quinta das Cruzes
Calçado do Pico 1
Open: Tuesday-Saturday 10am-12.30pm, 2-6pm.
Gardens open Tuesday-Saturday 10am-6pm

Museu Municipal
Rua da Mouraria
Open: Tuesday-Friday 9am-8pm, Saturday & Sunday 12noon-6pm

Museu Photographia Vicentes
Rua da Carreira 43
Open: Mon-Friday 2-6pm

Museu de Arte Sacra
21 Rua do Bispo
Open: Tuesday-Saturday 10am-12.30pm, 2.30-5.30pm. Closed holidays

São Francisco Wine Lodge
Avenida Arriaga 28
9003 Funchal
☎ 742121/741278
Open: Monday-Friday 9am-7pm, Saturday 9am-1pm. Tours Monday-Friday at 10.30am, 3.30pm

Churches

Baptist Church
Rua Cidade de Honolulu 9
(Between Rua Pedro José Ornelas and Rua Sidónio Pais)
Service: Sunday 6pm (English)
☎ 34484 (info)

English Church (CE)
Rua do Quebra Costas 18
☎ 22 0674
Services: Sunday 8am, 11am;
Wednesday 11am

Ingreja do Colégio
Mass: Sauturday 5pm, Sunday
10am, 12noon, 7pm
Open: daily 5-6pm and during
services

Santa Clara Convent Church
33/7 Rua de São Pedro
Open: 10am-12noon, 3-6pm

Scottish Kirk
Open: 9.30am-12.30pm, 2-4pm and
during services
Services: Sunday 12noon, 8pm
(Portuguese)

Sé (cathedral)
Rua do Aljube
Mass: Saturday 6.15pm, Sunday
8am, 9am, 11am

Public Transport
Information booths for Funchal
town buses at: Shopping Centre
Bom Jesus, Rua 31 de Janeiro 81,
stand 9 and Avenida das Comunidades Madeirenses. 7-day tourist
pass available, or pay on the bus
(more expensive).

Buses to Tourist Sites:
Jadim Botânico: 29, 30, 31
Lido: 1, 2, 3, 4, 6, 35
Monte: 20, 21
Museu da Cruzes: 15A
Pico do Barcelos: 9, 12
Quinta do Pahheiro Ferreiro
 Garden: 36

Tourist Information Office
Avenida Arriaga 18
9000 Funchal
☎ 229057

Boat Trips
The following all set off from
Funchal Marina

Albatroz sailing boat
☎ 9991454
Day cruise 10am-5pm, evening
cruise 7.30-9.30pm

Costa do Sol, LDA
☎ 38530/24390
Boat trips from Funchal to the
Desertas, Câmara de Lobos, Ponta
de São Laurenço, Ribeira Brava,
Ponta do Sol, Calheta, Baía d'Abra,
Machico, Cabo Girão

For big game fishing contact
Mr Rodrigues
☎ 225250

Festivals
February/Early March
Carnival

End of April/May
3-day flower festival

End of May & June
Music Festival

June 23-4
São Joãa da Ribeira

September
Wine Festival

1 May
Santa Maria Maior
Festival of St James

8-25 December
Christmas Festival
Special street and shop displays,
fireworks

30December-1 January
Festas de São Silvestre

2
GARDENS & MOUNTAINS

There are a number of places to visit on the outskirts of Funchal, especially the gardens for which the island is noted. These all need transport, but they are well served by bus, or a taxi could be hired. The highest mountains on Madeira are north of the capital and they can be explored by tours starting from Funchal.

The **Jardim Botânico** or 'official' botanical garden stands a little further up the slopes in the north-east of the town in Caminho do Meio. Take a bus with Jardim Botanico or Romeiros on the destination board and stroll through the marvellous gardens which are said to contain all the plants and flowers, bushes and trees which grow on Madeira. All species are labelled in Portuguese and Latin and, again, the gardens afford excellent views of the town and beyond. The gardens overlooks one of the spectacular viaducts on the new ring road round Funchal as it soars over the steep valley of the Ribeira de João Gomes and then plunges through the mountainside in twin tunnels. In the original house, the Quinta Bom Successo, which was once lived in by the family who owned Reid's Hotel, is a small museum of plant, animal and geological specimens, but they are displayed in a very old-fashioned manner, poorly labelled and with no descriptions.

The nearby **Jardim dos Loiros** is a tropical bird garden also worth a visit. Beautifully coloured parrots are among the principal attractions. They originate from primeval forests in all parts of the world and are also bred here. If you have the time a return to Funchal could be made on foot down the narrow but steep Caminho do Meio and Rua da Rochina.

About 200yd below the Botanical Gardens is **Jardim Orquídea**, where over 300 different species and over 3,000 different varieties of orchid may be see. Another orchid centre is at **Quinta da Boa Vista**,

46

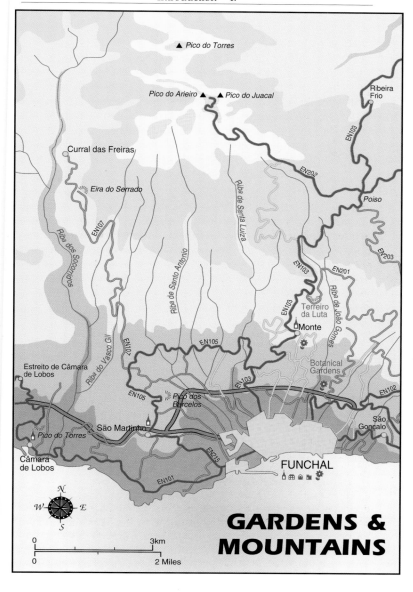

▲ Pico do Torres

Ribeira Frio

Pico do Arieiro ▲ ▲ Pico do Juacal

EN103

Curral das Freiras

EN202

Eira do Serrado

Poiso

Riba de Santa Luiza

EN203

Riba dos Socorridos

EN107

EN103

EN201

Riba de Santo Antonio

EN103

Riba de João Gomes

Terreiro da Luta

Monte

Riba do Vasco Gil

EN107

EN105

Botanical Gardens

Estreito de Câmara de Lobos

EN105

EN103

EN102

Pico dos Barcelos

São Gonçalo

São Martinho

Pico do Torres

Câmara de Lobos

EN215

EN101

FUNCHAL

N
W — E
S

0   3km
0   2 Miles

GARDENS & MOUNTAINS

5 minutes drive east of the centre of Funchal, but it is not easy to find and a taxi is advisable. The main season for orchids is January to May.

The **Quinta do Palheiro Ferreiro Gardens**, 7km (4 miles) northeast of Funchal on the road to Camacho, are usually known in tourist guides as 'Blandy's Gardens'. They consist of 12ha (30 acres) of parkland and are for most visitors the pearl in Funchal's botanical collection, with the added bonus of some fine views. The villa is owned by the English Blandy family and so the garden may only be visited in the morning from Monday to Friday. Planted with subtropical species collected from all around the world over the past 200 years, the gardens are laid out partly in the English, partly in the French style. (See Walk 3 to Babosa and Monte.)

One of the most popular excursions from Funchal is to **Monte**, a hillside village and place of pilgrimage, situated at 550m (1,800ft) above sea-level and 6km (4 miles) to the north of the city on the mountain road to Faial. The town enjoys a beautiful location between plane and oak woods, in an area favoured around the turn of the century when Monte was fashionable as an exclusive health resort with large estates and sanatoriums where the rich and ailing lived. Until it closed in 1939 following a fatal boiler explosion, you could travel to Monte from Funchal on a funicular railway, the track of which can stll be seen above the village's formal gardens. The famous downhill 'sledge ride' starts a little further to the west, above the Rua da Santa Luzia.

The twin towers of the church of Senhora do Monte, the island's patron saint, dates from the eighteenth century, although it is said to have been built on the foundations of an ancient chapel. This chapel is, in turn, said to have been founded around 1470 by the first two children born on Madeira, twins by the name of Adam and Eve. On 14 and 15 August, the church is at the centre of Madeira's biggest *Romaria*. Praying pilgrims climb up the seventy-four steps to the entrance on their knees. In a tabernacle above the main altar stands a venerated painting of the Virgin Mary. Studded with jewels, it is said to bestow miraculous powers. Charles I, the last Austrian emperor, who died in exile on Madeira in 1922, is buried in front of a side altar.

Below the church, and beside the tobogann run, are the **Monte Palace Tropical Gardens**, one of the finest on the island. Apart from the extensive splendid gardens with lakes, waterfalls, koi carp and exotic plants, there thirty panels of Portuguese tiles and a large collection of export oriental porcelain. The gardens are run by a private charitable foundation which is concerned with the conservation and restoration of works of art and historic monuments.

Following the streets in front of the church a little to the east leads to the **Old Monte Gardens**, and then to the **Babosas Balcony**. This panorama, by the bus stop for the return journey to Funchal, lies alongside a baroque-style chapel built in 1906.

About 3km (2miles) above Monte is the well-known viewpoint of **Terreiro da Luta** (876m/2,870ft). An attractive combination of cork oaks, acacia and eucalyptus trees provide the background for a magnificent view over Funchal, particularly in winter when many of the trees are bare. In the fifteenth century the painting of the Madonna of Monte who had miraculous powers was found here — at the spot where she is supposed to have appeared before a shepherdess.

Alongside a statue of Zarco, the island's discoverer, a marble statue, Nossa Senhora da Paz, honours the Virgin Mary in recognition of her help in bringing peace to the island during World War I, when a German submarine torpedoed British and French ships in Funchal harbour. The anchor chain from the French vessel serves as a rosary on the statue, having been carried up to the Terreiro da Luta near Monte in a special peace procession in 1927. In earlier days 'basket sledges' slid down from here to Funchal, but now they usually start in Monte.

Another viewpoint is **Pico dos Barcelos** at 364m (1,207ft) above sea-level and situated 4km (2½ miles) north-west of Funchal towards Curral das Freiras above the main hotels. This location offers a breathtaking view in all directions. (See Walk 2.) Take a detour on the return journey via **São Martinho** with its large modern church, a landmark clearly visible from some distance away. The view from here gives a clear overall impression of the town.

From one end of São Martinho the Caminho do Amparo leads down to the coast road above the Club Naval, while the main road at the other end becomes Rua do Dr Pita and joins the coast road above Reid's Hotel. The quieter Caminho do Nazaré runs parallel but a little further to the west and joins the Caminho da Casa Branca (linking Rua do Dr Pita with the coast road) above the Lido, the island's biggest swimming pool and park.

A viewpoint on the eastern side of the city is the **Miradouro do Pináculo**, 250m (820ft) above sea-level and 5½km (3½ miles) along the road to Caniço, where the view over Funchal is magnificent. On the return journey to the centre, follow the road a little deeper into the suburb of São Conçalo and take the Caminho Velho do Ribeira Seco and the Rua Lazareto to the old fishing quarter near the church of São Maria Maior and the small São Tiago fort.

Preparing for the downhill sledge ride from Monte

Monte Palace Tropical Gardens

Orchids are a Madeiran speciality

Early morning view from the Pico do Arieiro

Tours From Funchal

The following three tours from Funchal cover the main features of the island: a mountain, a valley and a fishing village. Each one needs only half a day (apart from time taken for walks), while the traveller in a hurry could take a taxi or use a hire car and take in all three in one day. The routes given here provide an opportunity to see the 'other' side of Madeira where forests alternate with terraced farmland. In some places, acacia and hydrangea line the country roads but the sea and mountains are nearly always in sight.

PICO DO ARIEIRO

※ A journey to **Pico do Arieiro** (1,810m/5,939ft) could be the continuation of an excursion to Monte and the Terreiro da Luta (8.7km/5½ miles from Funchal). A good 5km (3 miles) beyond in the direction of Faial, just after the pine forests of the Poiso pass (1,412m/4,630ft) the road branches off left to the Ariero. The summit stands about 7km (4½ miles) from the weather station, making a total of 21½ km (13½ miles) from Funchal.

So that the weather does not spoil your trip, ask your hotel receptionist to ring up the weather station. Clouds will spoil the visit as will a warm pullover left in the hotel room! Those who stay overnight at the *pousada* near the summit may experience sunrise with just the tops of the peaks showing though a sea of clouds — a sight once seen never to be forgotten.

※ Just before the end of the road, almost opposite the *pousada,* is a path to the Miradouro do Juncal (15 minutes return). The view from here extends over the Metade valley as far as the north coast, but a 20 minute walk from the car park on the summit of the Pico do Arieiro in the direction of Pico Ruivo is well worth the extra effort. It follows

※ the Panorama Path, as it is called, to the 'Eagle's Lair', **Miradouro do Ninho da Manta**, where harsh and rugged mountain landscapes dominate and where visitors can peer into fissures in the earth's crust and can try to imagine the strength of the forces which created the island millions of years ago. Yet on the steep rock faces that these forces left behind, soil accumulated and vegetation sprouted. Note the contrast between the lush greenery of the deep valleys and the bare mountains. Madeira's mountains are a thrilling experience.

𝍏 The **Panorama Path** is probably the only extended and permanent hill path on the island. It links the Pico do Arieiro with Madeira's highest mountain, the **Pico Ruivo** (1,861m/6,100ft above sea-level), a walk that takes about 2 hours. (See Walks 18 and 19.)

Tall heathers grow on the sides of the ravines and valleys, hence the name of Pico Ruivo meaning 'Purple Peak'. The last stages of the path are quite steep. Do not underestimate the effects of high altitude, especially on those who have come straight up from sea-level. Drinks are available from a small café at the summit.

CURRAL DAS FREIRAS

This trip is best done along with a visit to Pico dos Barcelos. About 12km (7½ miles) further on along the EN107 mountain road is the **Eira do Serrado** pass (1,026m/3,365ft), where a viewpoint offers a stunning view down to **Curral das Freiras** (Nun's Corral) in the valley of the Ribeira dos Socorridos. This was once believed to be the crater of an extinct volcano, but it is now thought that the softer tufa rock here was eroded more easily by the river. In 1566 nuns from the Santa Clara convent in Funchal sought shelter here from pirates who were attacking the city.

Take the few minutes to walk to the summit and the platform, from where the Pico Ruivo can also be seen. Some 400m (1,300ft) below, the river flows through a narrow gorge. A tortuous footpath leads down to the village (45 minutes) but there is also a road (4km/2½ miles) with two tunnels each about 400m (1,300ft) long. Warning: walkers ought to carry a torch in the tunnel. If time permits, take the local bus to beyond the first tunnel and walk about 15m/16yd to the left for a splendid view into the valley below. Walk the rest of the way into the village and return to Funchal by bus (16km/10miles). (See Walks 21 and 22.)

CÂMARA DE LOBOS

To reach the fishing port of **Câmara de Lobos**, 9km (5½ miles) west of Funchal, take a route either via São Martinho, Quebradas and Vitória or along the coast road. The busy Estrada Monumental passes through Funchal's hotel district and then leads out of the town. Directly below the round volcanic cones on the right-hand side, the road cuts off the southern tip of Madeira, Ponta da Cruz (a cross stands on a rock).

Situated to the west of Câmara de Lobos, **Cabo Girão**, one of the highest cliff faces in the world (578m/1,900ft), is just about visible from here. 'Girão' means 'turn round', which is what João Gonçalves Zarco did when he saw the cliff on his 'voyage of discovery' in 1419. The cliff is an amazing sight. The bare rock plunges down into the sea while on the land side of the hill, there is either lush grass or terracing for cultivation.

Finally the road passes a cement factory and a power station, the only one on the island to use imported oil rather than hydroelectric

Câmara de Lobos from the terrace where Winston Churchill used to paint

power. At the foot lies Câmara de Lobos (see page 80). It is still a picturesque spot even if there are no sea-lions here as the name suggests. In the deep harbour, fishing boats are still pulled up on to the shingly beach or sometimes for safety in bad weather dragged over the slipway beyond the harbour wall. Houses cling to the slopes with many built on a plateau of rock on the western side of the town. Behind the church with its baroque interior, a viewing terrace offers clear views of Cabo Girão.

By driving about 1km out of the village along the EN215, a right turn leads to the *miradouro* at Pico da Torre with a fine view down onto Câmara de Lobos.

Additional Information

Places to Visit

Funchal outskirts
Jardim Botânico
Caminho do Meio
Open: daily 9am-6pm
Natural History Museum open:
daily 9am-12.30pm, 1.30-5.30pm

Jardim dos Loiros
Open: daily 9am-6pm

Jardim Orquídea
Rua Pita da Silva
37 Bom Sucesso
9000 Funchal
(200m below Botanical Gardens)
Open daily: 8am-6pm

Quinta da Boa Vista
Rua Luis Figueroa de Albuqueque
☎ 20468
Open: Monday-Saturday 9am-
5.30pm

Quinta do Palheiro Ferreiro Gardens
'Blandy's Gardens'
on road to Camacha
Open: Monday-Friday 9.30am-
12.30pm. Closed 1 January, Easter
Friday, 1 May, 25-25 December

Monte
Church of Nossa Senhora do Monte
Open: daily 8am-1pm and during
services

Monte Palace Tropical Gardens
Caminho do Monte 174
9000 Funchal
☎ 782339/742650
Open: Monday-Friday 9am-5pm

Old Monte Gardens
Quinta Nossa Senhora da Conceicão
Open: Monday-Friday 10am-6pm

Festivals

Curral das Freiras
Early November
Festa da Castanho (Chestnut
    Festival)

Monte
14-15 August
Feast of the Assumption
Pilgrims climb the steps of the
church on their knees

3

EASTERN MADEIRA

This and the following two chapters describe a route round the whole of the island, and while theoretically possible to do it in one day, it is not really a practical proposition. The route is therefore divided into stages which may be treated individually or combined to give longer tours.

Funchal-Machico (26km/16miles)

A round trip of the island usually starts from the east of Funchal along the road that most visitors use from the airport on their way into Funchal, or the other main holiday centre of Caniço. Leave Funchal behind on the winding road and look out over the sea on the right-hand side towards the Pico Montanha. Most tour coaches stop at the **Miradouro do Pináculo** (5.5km/3½miles) so that passengers can enjoy the view back over the suburb of São Gonçalo and Funchal itself.

One and a half kilometres (1mile) further on, a road forks off to Garajau, although the main access road is 2km (1¼ miles) further on near **Caniço**, the centre of this agricultural region (229m/750ft above sea-level and 9½km/6miles from Funchal). Apart from flowers, wine and exotic fruit, the cultivation of onions for export plays an important part in the local economy. The imposing church of the Madra de Deus (Mother of God), is well worth a visit. It dates from the sixteenth century and displays many features of Manueline architecture. The cemetery gives some insight into the way Madeirans feel about their late-departed loved ones. Many of the headstones and crosses bear photographs of the deceased.

The coast with the tiny villages of **Garajau** and **Caniço de Baixo** is 2-3km (1-2miles) away. (See Walk 5.) The area is so delightful that the tourist hotel trade and the owners of the villas have joined forces to create a tourist centre which is thoroughly recommended — away from the hustle and bustle of Funchal and yet close enough for the night life and cultural attractions. A walking holiday centre is based here as is a diving centre. Steps lead down the cliff-face to the sea. Twenty minute's walk to the north of Caniço de Baixo lies the shingle beach of **Reis Magos**. (See Walk 6.)

Cabo Garajau or Tern Cape occupies a prominent position at the south-eastern corner of the island. Countless pairs of terns nest in the brass-coloured rock. At the tip of the cape stands a statue of Christ, similar to one in Rio de Janeiro — it dates from 1927 and was constructed at the request of the bishop of Funchal. It is possible to see the island's capital from here and on a clear day the Desertas Islands.

It is a further 6½km (4miles) from Caniço to the small fishing port of **Porto Novo** and then another 4km (2½ miles) along an inland road to the coastal town of **Santa Cruz**. With a population of about 10,000, several buildings including the former and present town hall and the church of San Salvador date from the sixteenth century. The ceiling painting in the church has a three-dimensional effect and the choir vaulting is borne by twisted pillars. In the hinterland, sugar cane is the main crop with a number of vineyards and banana plantations. The fishermen here supply many zoos throughout Europe with live, tropical fish. Their boats rock up and down in the shallow waters beyond the shingles in the harbour bay.

A little further along the coast, to the left of the main road, lies the island's airport. The access road to the airport, about 21km (13miles) from Funchal and 5km (3miles) from Machico, forks off about 1½km (1mile) after Santa Cruz.

The next sizeable settlement is **Agua de Pena** with the popular luxury Atlantis Hotel and the top-class Matur holiday complex. Another holiday centre has also been established here which has links with Machico's Dom Pedro Hotel.

Just before **Machico**, a road leads off to the left to a viewpoint offering a splendid view over the Bay of Machico. The sand on the beach is a browny-grey colour and grainy, but as it is one of the island's few sandy beaches, many bathers may well be tempted. Adjoining the beach is a large football pitch, which is bordered on the town side by a promenade. To the disappointment of sunbathers and swimmers, the sun disappears behind the mountains in the afternoon.

The name 'Machico' refers to the story of Robert Machin and his lover Anna who, about 1348 were on board a ship from Bristol. A

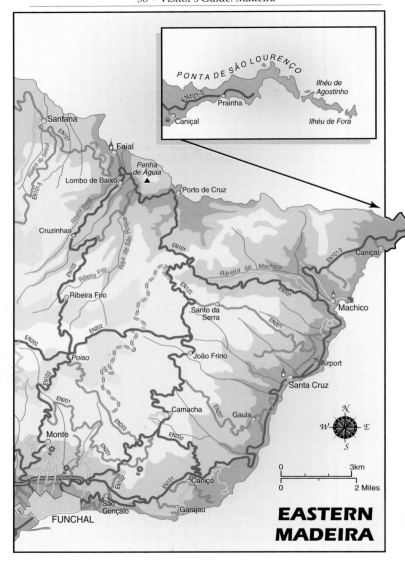

EASTERN MADEIRA

storm blew the ship off course and it finally landed here on the east coast of Madeira. The ship was wrecked and a new one had to be built before they could continue their voyage.

But Anna died and Robert did not survive for much longer and he was buried in the same grave as Anna, underneath a cedar tree. The crew eventually sailed their new ship to Morocco and ended up as slaves. Only one escaped and told of the unknown island which he called Machico after the Machins.

Almost a century later Henry the Navigator is said to have heard the story and sent Zarco and his companion Teixeira to search for the island. They landed at the same bay and found the grave under the cedar on the other side of the river. In their opinion, Madeira was a more suitable name for the island, but they kept Machico as the name for the place where Robert Machin was buried.

It was here that some of the first settlers to Madeira landed and they built the Capela do Senhor das Milagres, the 'Chapel of Miracles' on the site where they held their first mass. The town holds its festival on 8-9 October and visitors are welcome to join in the celebrations. On the slopes above the town, bonfires blaze, the streets are strewn with myrtle and rosemary branches and the townsfolk pass the night away singing, dancing, feasting and drinking. The procession on 9 October is the climax, marking the end of the

The Bird of Paradise flower is grown widely throughout Madeira

festivities. The town's original chapel was destroyed by a flood in 1803, but the old Manueline portal was incorporated into the new building. An old wooden cross said to be from the Machin's grave has been preserved.

The fishing quarter, on the other side of the river and thus often known as 'Banda d'Além', has developed into Machico's main shopping area but the fifteenth-century chapel of São Roque is worth seeking out. An interior wall contains an *azulejo* frieze telling the life of St Rochus. It begins on the right with his birth. The triangular fort of Nossa Senhora do Amparo (1706), hardly likely to deter any would-be invaders, stands guard over the town; it is now the local tourist office. Machico is the home port for Madeira's most important fishing fleet.

The larger half of Machico lies on the south side of the stone-banked river. It is dominated by the Hotel Dom Pedro at one end of the bay. The oldest church in this part of the town dates from the end of the fifteenth century and despite one or two alterations, including a tower made from red stone blocks, still shows features of the Manueline style. King Manuel himself donated the side portal with its slender marble pillars and also a figure of a saint. A statue of Tristão Vaz Texeira stands in front of the church. He was granted administrative rights over the eastern side of the island in the years immediately after its discovery.

A national school was established in Machico to retain and develop the skills needed for 'Madeiran Embroidery'. The material for their work is imported from Eire and Switzerland.

There is scope for many superb walks in the area around Machico. (See Walks 11, 12 and 16.) **Pico do Facho** (322m/1,050ft), some distance to the north, is a popular picnic site and viewpoint. The bus to Caniçal stops about 20 minutes walk away from the summit. For the return journey to Machico, either take a detour via Ribeira Seca (50 minutes) or descend to Caniçal (a good 90 minutes). Taking the opposite direction up to Caniçal is not recommended because of the incline. In earlier years a look-out post was situated on the Pico de Facho. When strange or perhaps enemy ships were sighted, a beacon was lit. On clear days the view extends from the São Lourenço peninsula and across to the neighbouring island of Porto Santo. The broad bay here is called the **Baia da Zarco**.

Alighting at the same bus stop on the main road, it is a 1¾ hour walk to the viewpoint on the **Boca do Risco** pass, 431m (1,415ft) above the northern coastline. To the west, the Eagle Rock at Faial can be seen and to the north east, the island of Porto Santo is sometimes visible.

DETOUR TO THE EASTERN TIP OF MADEIRA

The coast road from Funchal extends for another 13km (8miles) beyond Machico as far as the São Lourenço peninsula. On this 7km (4½ mile) stretch to Caniçal, the road passes through Madeira's longest tunnel (1,200m/1,300yd) which also has room for a *levada*.

Caniçal (population 2,000) is a small fishing port at the start of the island's north-eastern peninsula. Its importance has waned since the whaling station, just beyond the town, closed in 1981. Boatbuilding using traditional timber methods is now the principal activity in the town. (See Walks 13 and 15.)

'Baleia!' used to be a commonly heard cry, bringing the sleepy community to life. The look-out had sighted a whale, the men jumped into their boats and later returned with their booty, but that way of life has long since disappeared. The waters around the Madeiran archipelago are now protected and the environmental protection authorities have established The Museu de Baleia (Whaling Museum) in Caniçal. The scientists and tourists can gain an insight into the biology of the sea and its inhabitants, especially the threatened whale and also study the history of whaling which was so important to the fishermen. The locals may look rather forlornly at the 13m (42ft) model of a sperm whale, made from fibre glass, but those times are now past. Small whaling boats and harpoons are now manufactured for sale to tourists. The speciality in the local restaurants now is parrot fish fisherman-style!

Irrigation canals provide Caniçal and the surrounding area with the water necessary for the cultivation of fruit and vegetables. Only grass grows in the poorer soil further along the peninsula, where rain is infrequent, but the moisture of the winter months brings the wild grasses to life with a colourful display of blossom in the early spring.

The road ends after almost 6km (4miles) at Baia da Abra, where the last section of the rocky **São Lourenço peninsula** crumbles away into two islands. About halfway along the southern shores of the peninsula, the beach at **Prainha** stands out. With its black, volcanic sand, it is the only genuine beach in Madeira. A flight of steps descends the basalt cliffs and a small chapel seems to stand guard. Many of the visitors to this isolated corner come on boat excursions from Machico or even Funchal. A bus runs as far as Caniçal and then Prainha is a half-hour walk. Alternatively, take a taxi and then order it for the return journey. (See Walk 14.)

The north side of the peninsula is a haunt for geologists as petrified mussels and other fossils are often found on the shoreline. Bizarre cliff formations frequently confront the visitor to this section of the coast.

Machico-Santana (27km/17miles)

The main road around the island cuts off the eastern tip and heads inland before tracking the north coast. It first proceeds for 9km (5½ miles) through the cultivated Machico river valley up to the 620m (2,030ft) high **Portela pass**, where it meets the road north from Funchal via Camacha and Santo da Serra. The view from the east coast includes not only the high peaks at the heart of the island but also the northern coast where the Penha d'Aguia (Eagle Rock, 594m/ 1,948ft) dominates the landscape. To the right of the Penha d'Aguia and 6km (4 miles) from the Portela pass, between rugged cliffs and a shingle beach lies the old village of **Porto da Cruz.** Many magnificent, old-fashioned houses bear witness to the wealth derived from the fertile vineyards on the slopes of the inland valleys. (See Walks 17, 25 and 26.)

The road cuts to the south of the Penha de Águia (Eagle Rock), which lies 6km (4 miles) from Faial. The paths to the top are not easily negotiated. Just before Faial, the road across the island from Funchal via the Poiso pass and Ribeiro Frio (see page 84) meets the coast road. **Faial** occupies a low-lying site only 150m (490ft) above sea-level and is dominated by a large white church. (See Walk 27.)

The 6km (4 mile) journey on to Santana begins with a tight bend

Penha de Águia (Eagle Rock) towering over the village of Faial

Traditional thatched houses at Santana

through the countryside to the south. From a viewpoint at about the halfway point, Faial can be seen nestling beneath the Eagle Rock. On a clear day, the outlying rocks of the São Lourenço peninsula can also be distinguished as well as the island of Porto Santo.

Santana, at 414m (1,360ft) above sea-level, lies in the heart of one of Madeira's most fertile regions. The delightful thatched cottages seem to be involved in a year-round floral competition. Next to the town hall a group of them are open for visitors to see these traditional Maderian houses with their small living quarters on the ground floor and an upper level for storage. This type of building was once more widespread round the island, but now only those around Santana remain. Together with the many hedges covered in brightly-coloured blossom, they combine to create a village which must rank as one of the prettiest on the island.

Two roads lead up to the left and into the highlands: a new road ascends the **Achada do Teixeira** (about 10km/6½ miles), itself almost 1,600m (5,250ft) above sea-level. From here, a clearly marked footpath leads to the island's highest mountain, the Pico Ruivo (1,861m/6,100ft), a journey which will take about an hour. The footpath, the Panorama Path, continues beyond to the Pico do Arieiro (another 2 hours). Bear in mind that the walk back is considerably easier! Also, it is worth noting that early morning walkers will enjoy more of the sun than late risers. A longer walk is possible from the Pico Ruivo, the 'Purple Peak', to the Encumeada pass on the main road across the island (4½ hours). (See Walks 18, 19, 28.)

Before this new link from Santana up to the Achada do Teixeira was built, walkers had to take the steep path from Queimadas (1½ hours). The other route out of Santana, also very steep, climbs up from the coast road and ends in Queimadas (6km/4miles; junction 1.5km/1mile north-west of Santana).

Queimadas is the name of a state-run holiday village (900m/2,952ft) set amid lush vegetation by the Levada do Caldeirão and the customary footpaths. (See Walk 29.) The route to the east and the forester's lodge on the **Pico das Pedras** is easy (about 30 minutes). This is the spot where the road from Santana to Achada do Teixeira crosses. After another 30 minutes, a viewpoint in the **Cova da Roda** region offers a fine view over to the Eagle Rock near Faial and beyond to Madeira's eastern tip. (See Walks 30 and 31.)

Additional Information

Festivals

Caniçal
Third Sunday in September
Festival of Nossa Senhora de
    Piedade
Statue of Our Lady carried from
the chapel on Ponta de São
Lourenço in a procession of
decorated fishing boats

Santana
End of June
Festa das Tosquias (Sheep Shearing
    Festival)

July
Folklore Festival
Local music and dances

Machico
September 9
Nosso Senhor dos Milagres

October 8-9
Festival of the Miracles of Christ
Night-time procession with
bonfires and torches from the
Capela de o Senhor dos Milagres
(Chapel of Miracles) to Machico
parish church, to commemorate a
freak flood and avalanche in 1803
which swept away houses and the
chapel

Tourist Information Office

Machico
Fort of Nossa Senhora do Amparo

4
THE NORTH COAST

Santana-São Vicente (35km/22miles)

The road from Santana continues through magnificent country-side beneath the high mountains. Lined in places with hydrangea, it passes through narrow valleys with fertile south-facing slopes. **São Jorge** and its small seventeenth-century church with *azulejos* and rich baroque decorations lies some 9km (5½ miles) away.

The seventeenth-century church at São Jorge is one of the most interesting on Madeira

The north coast from the miradouro at Cabanas

The ceiling painting above the choir has the appearance of a relief. Vigia viewpoint on the Ponta de São Jorge promontory provides another panorama of the rocky northern coast: to the west stands Porto Moniz and to the east Porto Cruz. Turn off shortly beyond the edge of the village — the road is only metalled for a short distance and then walk for 15 minutes. From the centre of the village, allow 30 minutes.

Halfway between São Jorge and Arco de São Jorge is a *miradouro* at Cabanas with good views of the dramatic coastline. Here is a restaurant, motel, souvenir shop, a typical thatched house and stalls selling fruit.

Continuing along the coast road westwards, **Arco de São Jorge** (9km/5½ miles) has terraced slopes, but these are the result of earth movement and erosion. This is the start of another wine-producing region which extends as far as Ponta Delgada. The vines are trained along espaliers and are used in *sercial* wines. Broom hedges, a familiar sight throughout the island, cut across or border the vineyards in some places and serve as windbreaks.

Beyond Arco de São Jorge, the road winds inland in a 9km/5½ mile deep arc to cross the **Pôrco valley** upstream. It then returns to follow the coast but not until it has passed through one of the many road tunnels. This tunnel was built in 1954 and completed the stretch of road along the northern coast.

Boaventura, 7km/4½ miles beyond Arco de São Jorge and 3km/2miles before Ponta Delgada, is an important fruit-growing area and also provides much of the cane for the basket-making industry.

Ponta Delgada is a settlement scattered over a peninsula which was formed from a landslide. The homes of the peasant farmers, built on flat terraces, are close to their fields and gardens. The oranges from this part of the island are said to be particularly tasty. Below, a relatively large church perches on a low-lying rocky outcrop but it is rarely exposed to the sea spray. A seawater swimming pool has been built alongside the shingle beach in the small bay. On the first Sunday in September, the village is the scene for one of the *Romaria* followed by a celebration in honour of Christ, the 'Day of the Lord'.

The road follows the coast again and in places runs along the side of hills with sides which drop directly into the sea, providing a foretaste of the remaining section to Porto Moniz. It is a good 6km/4miles to **São Vicente** where a four-star hotel at the water's edge caters for the tourist trade. Even though São Vicente is principally a coastal town the attractive old part is just inland up the road which cuts across the island to Ribeira Brava. Once again, windbreaks have been constructed to protect the vines from the north winds. The painting on the ceiling in the village church is worth a quick look: it shows the village together with its church. Hereabouts the picturesque streets are pedestrianised with a variety of small shops.

It is at this point that the main cross-island link road heads south to Ribeira Brava (35km/22miles, see Chapter 6) through a changing agricultural landscape. At the mouth of the river and built into a large rock is a chapel which dates from 1696. Out of the village, on the road to Boca da Ecumeada, an unusual modern church, dedicated to the Virgin of Fatima, overlooks the village. Its disproportionately large tower dwarfs the rest of the building.

São Vicente-Porto Moniz (16km/10miles)

This part of the tour must rank as one of the most breathtaking stretches of road on the island, with hairpin bends alongside sheer drops to the sea — but there are good crash barriers all the way. First tunnels and then galleries to prevent rocks from cascading on to the road, for it should be borne in mind that the elements in this part of Madeira are much less hospitable than elsewhere.

After the first 7km (4½ miles) from São Vicente to Seixal, the landscape becomes wilder, crossing an impressive 'Devil's Valley' of luxuriant, but shady woodland and then waterfalls pour down over the cliffs. One such waterfall used to land on the road but a tunnel now protects motorists from the largest of them. A layby is sited nearby so that sightseers can view the waterfall and the tunnel.

Seixal lies at the centre of a small wine-producing region with some highly prized vintages on offer. Outcrops of rock around the tip of the peninsula and volcanic coastal rocks either side of the town are clearly visible. A detour can be made down to the picturesque small harbour.

Several longish walks climb the north-west slope of the Paúl da Serra plateau, beyond to Rabaçal and also up to the road which runs south-east in an arc from Porto Moniz. But a detour into this region, sometimes known as the Scotland of Madeira, is best undertaken from the south. (See Chapter 6.)

Ribeira da Janela, once the site of one of Madeira's four hydro-electric power stations, lies 6.5km/4miles past Seixal. In some places, the coast road perilously hugs the sides of hills which drop almost vertically into the sea, passing through yet more tunnels and then on beneath terraced, cultivated hillsides as at Ribeira da Janela itself. 'Janela' means window and refers to the gaping hole in the biggest of the rocky islets which occupy the mouth of the river (it cannot be seen from the bridge).

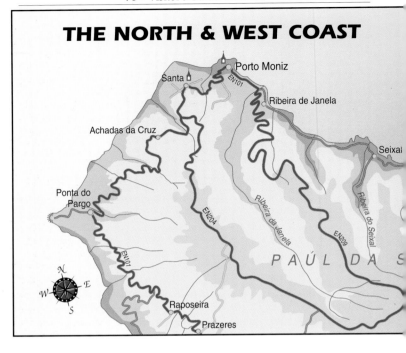

THE NORTH & WEST COAST

São Vicente

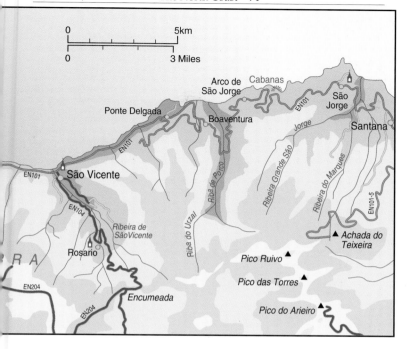

Rock pools at Porto Moniz

The road from Ribeira da Janela along the northern banks of the Janela river to the Paúl da Serra eventually meets up with the southern coast road between Canhas and Porto do Sol, but if you prefer take the better route on the southern side of the river. In any case no visitor to this region would turn back just before reaching journey's end on this popular west route — it is only another 2½km (1½ miles) to Porto Moniz. If using buses, complete the last part of this section on foot. They wait for 2 to 3 hours in Porto Moniz anyway.

Many visitors will be tempted by the natural swimming pool between the jagged lava cliffs below **Porto Moniz** (population 3,500). This cliff-top town, situated on the north-western tip of the island and the administrative centre for the north coast district, is one of the most picturesque spots on the island with many old houses and cobbled alleys. The church dates from the seventeenth century. The busy fishing port, once a whaling station, lies lower down where many of the restaurants are to be found, most of whom seem to cater for the tourist coaches which stop here. Numerous small sea water pools have been created here out of the rough black lava rocks. Nature seems to have made common cause here with both bathers and fishermen as this is the only sheltered place on the windy northern coast.

Porto Moniz is the furthest settlement from Funchal — a total of 103km (64miles) via the route described here and a further 100km (62miles) if following the coast road for the return journey. A full circuit of the island in one day is only a theoretical possibility and certainly not to be recommended. There are too many places to visit, sights to see and walks to enjoy.

It is therefore advisable to split the full island tour into two and to return to Funchal via the cross-country Ribeira Brava to São Vicente route — Funchal to Porto Moniz is a 70km (43mile) journey.

Returning from Porto Moniz via the south side of the Janela river across the wild and eerie Paúl da Serra plateau and then down to the southern coast road will save fuel and, with fewer bends, this route will reduce driver fatigue. Besides, there is no other way of experiencing Madeira's contrasting landscapes.

Additional Information

Festivals

Porto Moniz
July
Agricultural Festival & Cattle Show

Ponta Delgada
1st Sunday in September
Senhora Jesus ('Day of Our Lord')

5
THE WEST & SOUTH COAST

Porto Moniz-Calheta (44km/28miles)

From sea-level at the north-west corner of the island, the coast road veers inland and up into the hills, first to the south-west tip, then along the south side of the island and finally back to Funchal (100km/62miles). The first section from Porto Moniz to Calheta is not a popular route for visitors. This part of the island is quite isolated and the scenery, although still wild, is not as striking as the north coast. Much of the land is wooded, but farmers still manage to cultivate vegetables, fruit and cereals.

A few hairpin bends begin the steep climb out of **Porto Moniz** to about 500m (1,650ft). Two viewpoints break the ascent allowing the ※ sightseer two opportunities to look down over this unique juxtaposition of man and nature: water, rocks and spray set alongside the chequered pattern of fields separated by broom hedge.

Just under 5km (3miles) beyond Porto Moniz, stop off in the village of **Santa Maria Madalena** and visit the small church or **⌂** simply admire the minaret-style tower from the road. Two kilometres (1¼ miles) further on, the cross-country route via the Paúl da Serra plateau forks off to the east. Continuing to the south-west, at **Achadas da Cruz** 3km (2miles) further on, the road has already reached an altitude of 700m (2,300ft).

For the next 10km (6½ miles) the road descends into the south-western corner of Madeira with a lighthouse (375m/1,230ft) at the ※ end of the promontory, a little beyond the village of **Ponta do Pargo** (470m/1,541ft). 'Pargo' means dolphin after a huge dolphin which was caught in the coastal waters nearby. The lighthouse is the westernmost point of Madeira, and there are fine views of the sheer cliffs which are composed of layers of volcanic ash.

In this south-western corner of the island, many of the old customs

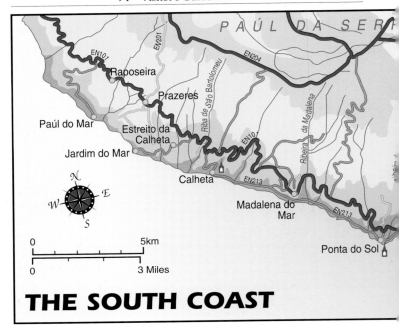

THE SOUTH COAST

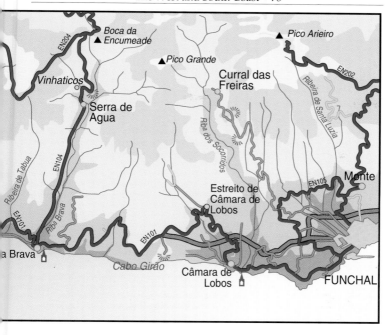

⇐ *The west of the island is less developed than the rest of Madeira*
An old sugar cane mill, restored as a picnic site, at Calheta

survive. More people in this region still wear the fine old costumes, usually just on Sundays and holidays. They are certainly not worn for the tourists but to remain faithful to long-standing traditions. At other times, women can still be seen carrying baskets or buckets on their heads and clothes are often washed in the nearby stream.

The road is very windy; time and again, it crosses streams and small rivers with fine views over the sea. Some 8km (5miles) beyond Ponta do Pargo, a side road branches off to Faia da Ovelha (3km/2miles), which then descends to the sea at **Paúl do Mar** (another 5km/3miles). The main route continues eastwards to **Prazeres** another 5km (3miles) further on. This village occupies an attractive site high up on a plain, part terraced and part wooded, with its houses huddled around a small church (621m/2,036ft above sea-level). It is an area popular with walkers, eg down to Paúl do Mar through a lush, steep-sided gorge. Roads head up to the Paúl do Serra as well as to fine vantage points looking out to sea.

Estreito da Calheta (339m/1,111ft) is another 4km (2½ miles) further on and just beyond, a road runs down to the sea at **Jardim do Mar** (5km/3miles).

After another 2km (1¼ miles) comes the turning to the coastal town of **Calheta**, 63km (39miles) in total from Funchal. It is the centre of the banana-growing and wine producing region. The village church has undergone many changes, but the old wooden ceiling in Manueline style is well maintained. A silver and ebony tabernacle presented by Manuel I is also of interest. (See Walk 35.)

The chapel of the Three Kings (*Reis Magos Capela*) on the road down to Calheta is also worth a visit. This sixteenth-century chapel remains almost completely untouched and houses a delightful wooden carving, a triptych of the Three Kings. The old cedar ceiling is also still in good condition and the bronze font is a fine example of the Manueline style. Down by the coast road a pleasant picnic site has been made alongside the preserved remains and machinery of a sugar cane mill, built in 1909 — along with an old steam roller and wine machinery in a park in Funchal it is one of the few examples of industrial archaeology on Madeira.

Continuing along the recently improved lower coast road with tunnels through the headlands, and passing through **Madelena do Mar** and **Ponta do Sol** to Ribeira Brava is actually much quicker than using the EN101 main road with its innumerable bends.

The main road continues east and after 1½km (1mile) a minor road heads north into the mountains, linking with the road across the Paúl da Serra to Porto Moniz (12km/7½ miles) before making its way to Rabaçal.

Calheta-Ribeira Brava (31km/19miles)

Climb the 3km (2miles) back to the main road where in the course of the first 7km (4½ miles) to Loreto, the turnings mentioned above to the highlands and to the hydro-electric power station are all signposted to Rabaçal. In the tiny village of **Loreto**, it would be worth stopping off to admire the chapel of the Holy Virgin with its striking Manueline battlements. The altar painting is of Flemish origin.

Some 1½km (1mile) beyond Calheta, at the foot of the Pico do Arco (876m/2,873ft) lies the village of **Arco da Calheta**. Continue along the main road for another 8km (5miles), passing above the coastal settlement of Madalena do Mar, before reaching the attractively-sited village of **Canhas** (330m/1,082ft) which is noted for the pretty costumes worn by villagers on special occasions. Just 2km/1¼ miles before the village, a road forks off to the left and snakes its way up to the Paúl da Serra plateau. The main road into the mountains turns off just 2km (1½ miles) after Canhas or a similar distance before the junction to Ponta do Sol. This road links with the cross-country route to Porto Moniz and is known as the 'Serra Road'.

The remaining 12km (7½ mile) section of the main road from Canhas to Ribeira Brava follows an undulating and twisting course with two side roads each 1km (over ½ mile) long down to the coastal villages of Ponta do Sol and Tabua. Sugar cane is grown in this region, as are bananas and, of course, grapes. It goes without saying that the southern side of the island enjoys protection from the wind and benefits from more hours of sun.

In **Ponta do Sol** (population 8,000), Moorish influence is clearly visible in the parish church's ceiling painting. The font finished in green glaze is also of interest. Both date from the sixteenth century. An unexpected treat awaits visitors to the Capela do Espirito Santo in the nearby village of **Lombada da Ponte do Sol**. This chapel was originally built by João Esmeraldo, a friend of Christopher Columbus who owned a large sugar-cane plantation nearby. On an old house opposite the chapel is the the coat-of-arms of the Esmeraldo family. The chapel was restored in the seventeenth century and demonstrates the simple elegance that characterised the merging of Renaissance and baroque styles. On the outside the portal is note-worthy, while inside special features include several gilded baroque altars as well as *azulejo* friezes illustrating the virtues. (See Walk 34.)

While driving the last few kilometres of the road into **Ribeira Brava**, it soon becomes clear that the visitor is leaving the island's 'Wild West' behind and is rapidly approaching that part of Madeira which has kept in step with twentieth century. It is here that the main road over the mountains to São Vicente (25km/16miles; see page 85)

Pointsettia growing by the roadside near Ponta do Sol

Ribeira Brava from the miradouro *above the town*

veers inland. There is also a three-star hotel and a centre for walking holidays. Ribeira Brava has thus become the gateway to the west — not just the coast and but also the highland region.

Situated in a beautiful spot, between sea and mountains, it draws many visitors and even the shingle beach has its attractions. A tunnel leads from the town, where the small market-place is decorated with black stones, to the fishing harbour.

By the seafront car park and the fruit and vegetable market is an old watch tower, which is decorated every Christmas with an ❄ elaborate nativity scene. Most of the houses, like almost everywhere else, have red roofs. The church, which has been restored a number of times, has a side chapel with a magnificent pulpit and a finely ⛪ decorated font. The pointed bell-tower is finished with black and white tiles. Behind the church are narrow streets with small shops selling all manner of goods.

Before leaving Ribeira Brava, visit the *miradouro* on the Funchal road for a splendid view down over the roof-tops of the town.

Ribeira Brava-Funchal (31km/19miles)

The climb east starts with more hairpin bends. After 4½km (2¾ miles), there is a magnificent view over Cabo Girão. Within 1½km (1mile) at the village of **Campanário** the road reaches a height of 300m (980ft). The small church was built in 1683. Quinta Grande 5km ⛪ (3miles) further on, stands at 525m (1,722ft) above sea-level and in the uplands to the north there are good *levada* walks. (See Walk 33.)

After a further kilometre (½ mile) at Cruz da Caldeira (bus stop), a side road runs down to the *miradouro* at **Cabo Girão**. This magnifi- ❄ cent cliff (578m/1,900ft) is said to be the highest cliff in Europe. Needless to say, there is a superb view along the jagged coastline, with Funchal in the distance and the Atlantic waves brushing the rocks at close quarters. One remarkable feature along this rugged coastline are the pockets of green — some natural, some man-made — which despite the sea flourish among the cracks and crevasses on the smallest patch of soil, level or not. (See Walk 32.) 🚶

Four kilometres (2½miles) beyond the turning to the cape, at the end of a terraced valley, lies the wine village of **Estreito de Câmara de Lobos**, a possible starting point for tours into the island's interior. (See Walk 20.) Partly passable by car, the 6km (4mile) drive to **Jardim da Serra** (750m/2,460ft) is rewarded by a splendid view into a 100m (325ft) deep mountain valley. Serious walkers can get a little further by taxi, so that a hike to the Curral das Freiras is viable. (See Walk 21.) 🚶

The main road continues through fairy-tale countryside with

terraced hillsides at the heart of one of the most fertile regions on the whole island. Many wine lovers regard the madeira from this region to be the finest. The vines are trained using the espalier method and the grapes are used in the production the *sercial* variety.

Picturesque **Câmara de Lobos** at the foot of Cabo Girão is a further 6km (4miles) further on and is often chosen as a subject by painters. Winston Churchill came here to paint and draw, often choosing scenes of the small bay with its remarkable lava breakwater and the brightly-coloured fishing boats with dark sails.

The place is now an important centre for deep-sea fishing and although it only has a population of 15,000, it seems to have the highest numbers of children. There is nowhere else on Madeira where tourists are pestered so much by child beggars. Despite its picturesque appearance the houses near the port are poor and run down. The town is named after the sea-lions which once sunned themselves in the bay. The *espada* or scabbard fish is king here now and should be sampled — it tastes simply delicious!

The small church on higher ground is a good example of richly ornamented eighteenth-century baroque. Women are sure to notice the Madeira embroidery available and a school has also been established here to preserve this ancient tradition.

The mountain stream, Ribeira dos Socorridos, which flows into the Atlantic a little to the east of the town, is worthy of mention and not just for its wild beauty. Footpaths and roads follow the stream on both sides for quite a way inland. *Socorridos* means 'survivors', as a group of islanders used the stream to escape from a major forest fire.

Many visitors to the island make Câmara de Lobos the destination for their first trip out of Funchal (see Chapter 2) and so it is an appropriate place for the final stop on this island tour. **Funchal** is now only 9km (5½ miles) away, making a round trip of 200km (124 miles) in all, not including detours. Many drivers may prefer the inland route via São Martinho to the busy coast road which leads straight into the heart of the congested capital.

Additional Information

Festivals

Caheta
September 7-8
Nossa Senhora do Loreto

Ponto do Pargo
September
Festa da Pêra (Pear Festival)

Ribeira Brava
29 June
Festival of St Peter (São Pedro)
Small boat decorated with flowers carries the saint's image to the church

October
Festival of Madeiran Musical Bands

6

ACROSS THE ISLAND

Funchal-Machico (30km/19miles)

Strictly this first cross-country link road does not cross the island, but runs diagonally inland as far as Machico. It is a variation to the route in Chapter 3 and may be mainly of interest to visitors to the São Lourenço peninsula. (See map page 58.)

Leave Funchal in a north-easterly direction and pass the Quinta do Palheiro Ferreiro. **Camacha** (700m/2,300ft) with a population of 6,500 is situated some 10km (6½ miles) from Funchal and is the home of the Funchal flower sellers, who are famous for their colourful costumes. But it is not just flower growing that provides the town with its livelihood. The profitable basket-making industry is also based here and it is possible to see inside the workshops (although much is made by people working at home) and, of course, to buy the products — those made here are said to be the best on the island and the prices are very reasonable too. In the large showroom is virtually ✳ everything that you can think of — and many others that you never even imagined could be made from wickerwork — from baskets and furniture to animals and even an almost life-size boat! The origins of this industry goes back to a time when wicker baskets were used to hold Madeiran fruit destined for overseas markets.

During the last century when Madeira was almost counted as another 'British colony', British settlers often chose the area around Camacha with its wooded upland landscape for their summer residences. Fields of fruit and flowers cover the green slopes, making ideal walking country. (See Walks 4, 7, 8.)

On a wooded plain 11km (7miles) beyond Camacha stands **Santo da Serra** (675m/2,214ft). Although it is noted for its delicious apples, other fruit and vegetables are grown here. Many wealthy residents of Funchal have weekend houses in or near the town as the tempera-

Wickerwork in the showrooms at Camacha

Locally made souvenirs at Ribeira Frio

The neatly laid-out trout hatchery at Ribeira Frio

tures are a little cooler here during the summer. Among the amenities for visitors include tennis courts, children's playgrounds and picnic sites and there are some fine walks too, eg to the Pico do Suna and Lamaceiros or even further afield across to Ribeiro Frio or down to Santa Cruz. (See Walks 9 and 10.)

Other attractions include a wild animal reserve and a golf course. The bigger hotels are affiliated to the golf club so that guests can play golf at no extra cost. There are fine views from the golf course down to the coast and across to Porto Santo and the Desertas.

From Santo da Serra it is only another 5km (3miles) to the Portela pass and 9km (5½ miles) through a fertile valley down to **Machico**, the oldest place on the island. However, the short cut from Santo da Serra to the Machico road saves 5km (3miles).

Funchal-Faial(32km/20miles)

The first section of this tour together with a detour to the Arieiro is only a short excursion from Funchal and is described in 'Tours from Funchal' (Chapter 2). Monte (550m/1,804ft) lies 6km (4miles) from the capital and **Terreiro da Luta** (876m/2,873ft) just under 3km (2miles) further on. There are some fine views back over Funchal.

Climb another 5km (3miles) to the **Poiso pass** (1,412m/4,631ft) which is 14km/9miles from Funchal. Stop and have a good look at the scenery! A few hundred metres north of the pass turn off right towards Machico or turn left for a breathtaking drive to one of Madeira's highest peaks, the Pico do Arieiro (1,810m/5,939ft). A detour to the mountain top (7km/4miles) will offer not only superb views over the north and north-west of the island, but also an insight into the volcanic origins of this Atlantic mountain range.

Ribeiro Frio, 5km (3miles) downhill from Poiso, lies in a wooded valley (800m/2,624ft) rich in vegetation and, with its restaurants and large souvenir shop, is a popular destination for day-trips from Funchal. Just before the village is a collection of indigenous Madeiran plants — the tree ferns, some exceeding 10m (33ft) in height, are particularly impressive.

On the opposite side of the road the Ribeiro Frio, or 'Cold River', feeds the pools of a government-run trout farm. Visitors are free to wander round the pools, in a very attractive setting, to see the fish in the various stages of their growth. The farm not only supplies trout to restaurants in the area, but also stocks other rivers with fish.

Also signposted just below the village is an half-hour walk to the *miradouro* at **Balcões** (870m/2853ft). The peaks of the Arieiro, the Torres and the highest mountain on the island, Pico Ruivo (1,861m/

6,100ft) can all be seen assuming visibility is good. In the opposite direction the distinctive Eagle Rock near Faial is visible. Some 300m/980ft below is the Metade valley. (See Walks 23, 24, 25.)

The road then descends into the fertile Metade valley and then to **Cruzinhas** on the other side of the river. Deep gorges gape on both the left and right. Further below to the right, the church of São Roque do Faial can be seen perched on a ridge between the two valleys. The Eagle Rock looms ahead and 5km (3miles) from Cruzinhas, the road meets the Machico to Santana route (Chapter 3) just outside **Faial**.

Ribeira Brava-São Vicente (24km/14miles)

This cross-island link is generally used for journeys to Porto Moniz, but also serve as a short cut or an opportunity to admire the beautiful scenery. The road runs along two river valleys, one up and one down. The sides of both valleys are lined either with craggy rock formations and primeval woodland or else they are terraced and farmed. Fine views extend over the island with insights into the creative power of man and nature. It will also be clear to visitors how the north coast differs from the south.

The road from Ribeira Brava is one of the few on the island (apart from the new roads round Funchal and to the airport) that are level and where you can get into top gear! Just 7km/4½miles from the coast lies the pretty village of **Serra de Agua** (350m/1,150ft). In places poplars mark the river bank. The road becomes steeper over the next 6km (4miles), passes the beautifully-situated Pousada dos Vinháticos and then climbs steeply over the 1,007m (3,302ft) high **Encumeada pass** with an extensive viewpoint. On a clear day you can see both of the island's mountain ranges to right and left and also both coastlines with blue sea in the background.

Several long and short walks start either from the pass or from the *pousada* 3km (2miles) away. The Ridge Walk descends from the east and links with Encumeada here. Its starting point is the Pico do Arieiro and follows the Panorama Path as far as the Pico Ruivo at 1,861m (6,100ft) and the highest peak on the island (2 hours). From there, it continues its way over more peaks with views both to north and south, as well as some gentle and steep inclines (allow at least 4½ hours). There are two turnings off the main path — one to Curral das Freiras to the south and another along the Pôrco valley which leads down to the north coast. (See Walks 19, 20, 22.)

Tear yourself away from the Encumeada pass with its magnificent views and descend the 11km (7miles) to sea-level near São Vicente. Rosario, at about halfway, has a chapel with a tall bell-tower which can be seen from the edge of the Paúl-da-Serra plateau. The road runs along a hardened lava outflow which once almost blocked the northern Ribeira Grande river valley.

Both starting and finishing points on this tour are described in the circular tour: Ribeira Brava in Chapter 5 and São Vicente in Chapter 4. Good hotel accommodation is available in both towns.

The Paúl da Serra

The **Paúl da Serra,** a barren moorland, extends westwards from the Encumeada pass above a deep gorge. The main route across this region starts as a new road which climbs dramatically even higher from the pass, eventually joining the main EN101 coast road southwest of Porto Moniz. Also a number of minor roads climb onto the plateau from the south coast. Translated, Paúl da Serra means 'mountain marshland' but more accurately, it is barren moorland with moss and brambles, ferns and heathers. Small wild horses used to roam here, but now there are just a few cows grazing on the meagre grasses. Although the average altitude of the plateau is in the region of 1,350m (4,430ft), humps and rocky projections can increase the height to 1,640m (5,400ft). Mist often shrouds the desolate terrain, and the region is frequent compared, with justification, to Scotland.

Many mountain walkers who really want to get to know Madeira, follow first the Ridge Walk and then on the second day, make for

The Janela valley near Rabaçal on the Paúl da Serra

Rabaçal. Although the route starts with some fairly steep inclines both up and down, it then becomes less demanding (as long as mist does not descend!). There are mountain shelters and road links to the south coast and also to the far north-west corner of the island. Many walkers camp here but strictly speaking it is not allowed although usually tolerated. The path across the Paúl-da-Serra plateau runs from the Bica da Cana, the peak opposite the Encumeada pass, to the statue of Christ on the road to Canhas. The subsequent mountain walk to Rabaçal follows the Levada do Paúl (see Walks 36 and 37).

The only settlement on the Paúl de Serra is **Rabaçal**, a popular holiday village and destination for outings, and much loved by Madeirans. It lies just beneath the plateau close to the source of the island's longest river, the Janela, which, fed by the waters of countless streams, works its way northwards to the sea. Tree heaths and thick laurel woodland grow wild in the surrounding area, close to the point where two levadas meet and also the holiday village. The road down to the village is steep, winding and single track with no crash barriers, descending into a deep ravine.

The **Risco Waterfalls** are only an easy 20 minute walk away, but allow an hour to get to the 25 Fontes. This route is not so simple and there are some gentle gradients, but eventually the path reaches the narrow valley where the **25 Fontes** (one large and one small waterfall) cascade down, forming an inviting pool. (See Walks 38 and 39.)

It is possible to take another *levada* from Rabaçal, following it round in an arc via Florença to reach **Loreto** on the main road (1½ hours). (See Walk 40.)

Up on the 'Serra road', the water tank at the fork to Rabaçal is the starting point for a walk along the Levada da Paúl to the east to the striking **Cristo Rei** (statue of Christ). It is situated quite close to the main road from Canhas to Serra do Paúl and is well-known to taxi drivers as a picking-up point. (See Walk 36.)

A little above Cristo Rei and to the east a disused track leads to the central area of the plateau, the panorama at **Bica da Cana** (1,620m/5,310ft). (See Walk 37.) Further east a deep valley divides the higher part of the island from the lower part. The main north-south link road follows the course of this valley over the Encumeada pass (1,007m/3,300ft) from Ribeira Brava to São Vicente.

Additional Information

Festivals

Camacha
October
Festa da Maçã (Apple Festival)

Traditional music, processions and drinking of *cidra* (apple cider)

7
PORTO SANTO
& THE OTHER ISLANDS

Porto Santo lies just 37km (23miles) north-east of Madeira and is best known for its sandy beaches. The islanders here are sometimes the butt of a joke among Madeirans as Porto Santo can sometimes be abbreviated to PS or a post script to the main island, but Madeira cannot boast of golden beaches several kilometres long, often completely deserted.

There are two hotels, several *pensions* and also holiday homes to rent or buy. But there is no 'night-life' to speak of, just a friendly atmosphere and not much else to do apart from sit in the sun, enjoy the gentle breeze, swim, dive, snorkel, waterski, fish, go horseriding or take a ride on a horse and carriage. Most of the long-stay visitors to Porto Santo are Madeirans with only a few continental Europeans who come in search of total relaxation.

A new speedboat link with Funchal has brought an increase in the number of day-trippers to the islands, mainly tourists wanting a break from Funchal's hustle and bustle and a taste of Porto Santo's simple life. Ox carts, no longer seen on Madeira, have been brought over to Porto Santo and are a favourite means of transport, although they are usually pulled by horses. On the other hand, it is possible to rent mountain bikes, ideal for youngsters who want to see the island.

The island is 14km (9miles) long and a good 6km (4miles) wide. Of the 4,000 inhabitants, about half live in the island's main town or along the sandy south coast, also known as Porto Santo, although it is actually called **Vila Baleira**. Old-fashioned white-washed houses surrounded by palm trees and flowers give the impression of a colonial settlement. The tourist office opposite the post office will supply visitors with information on accommodation etc and also suggestions for walks. The only tourist attraction is the house behind the old church in the town hall square, where Christopher Columbus lived around 1480. It has been renovated and now houses the museum. He married one of the daughters of the first governor of Porto Santo, the famous navigator Bartolomeu Perestrelo. The wedding is said to have taken place in Machico but the couple later moved to Funchal. It is also thought that their son Diego was born on the island.

The scenery on Porto Santo is quite different from that of Madeira as the underlying volcanic rock is covered with chalky sandstone. The hillsides are terraced but there are no '*palheiros*' as cattle are left to graze outside. The island is extremely dry and treeless. Sandy plains occupy land in the interior and of the rocky peaks which surround them, the Pico do Facho in the north-east is the highest (507m/1,660ft).

Nevertheless, grapes, melons, fruit and vegetables, even cereal crops all grow here, but the rainfall is not reliable and sometimes drought destroys everything. On the route to the airport attempts at afforestation can be seen. It is hoped that trees and bushes will halt soil erosion on the island.

Almost everywhere, islanders can be seen carrying water. The men carry buckets hanging from a yoke, while women often balance jugs, or other goods on their heads. Life is a struggle for an island population with a very poor standard of living, but nevertheless, the people and their homes are spotlessly clean and their lean cattle well-cared for. The landscape is dotted with the remains of windmills which at one time brought life and movement to an otherwise barren scene, but now only two are in working order.

The view from the well-proportioned volcanic cone of **Pico da Castelo** (437m/1,433ft) covers the whole of the island and on a clear day Madeira should be visible, although a heat haze is likely to spoil the view. The peak is accessible by road and island explorers will find there the remains of fortifications built in the sixteenth century to protect the locals from pirates.

The airport runway seems to be longer than a small island would normally require, but it was built to such specifications so that it could be used by NATO planes in emergencies. At the northern end of the runway lies the subject of a geology lesson. **Fonte da Areia**, 'the spring in the sand', is certainly worth a visit. See how part of the inner structure of the earth's crust was forced to the surface and then broken up by elemental forces, thus exposing the various rock strata.

The beautiful sandy beach extends for about 9km (5miles) on the gently curved south side of the island and a fine view over the full length of the beach is possible from the village of **Portela**, 2km (1¼ miles) east of Vila Baleira. At the easternmost point of the island,

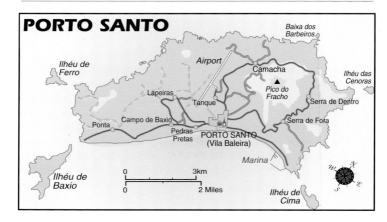

PORTO SANTO

Ponta da Calheta, the sandy beach ends and the shore is dominated by some bizarre basalt rock formations. The coast line on the north side of the island is rocky.

A boat trip round the island is a must for good sailors, otherwise you could make enquiries about a circular tour of the island by donkey! Then the island's own mineral water will taste even better and you might start to believe in its healing powers — at the very least it revives weary sun-drenched spirits and keeps local industry

In contrast to Madeira, Porto Santo has superb beaches

in business. Whatever else, it is the only water on the island that is safe to drink.

Many people say that the sand also has special healing powers. Maybe … but if you are intending to make Madeira your next holiday destination, then plan to spend at least some of your time on Porto Santo and have two holidays in one.

The Desertas

The Desertas Islands and the more remote Selvagens are not inhabited. In fact, the **Selvagen Islands** are over 250km (150miles) away from Madeira and geographically closer to the Canary Islands. In the summer, fishermen live there and botanists visit from time to time to undertake research. The islands have also attracted a rather disreputable group who kill certain nesting sea birds for their dried flesh — regarded by some as a delicacy.

The **Desertas** or the Deserted Islands can be seen from Madeira and are situated some 28km (17miles) to the south-east. There are three islands, Chão, Bugio and in between them the biggest Deserta Grande, a 500m (1,640ft) high basalt table. It is 10km (6½ miles long) and only 500m wide. Steep cliffs dominate the shoreline and reefs close by present a danger for boats, so a calm sea is essential for anyone seeking to land. However, only scientists and researchers are given permits to land and just for certain purposes, for example, to study an unusual species found only on these islands — a large, highly poisonous spider and one of the biggest in Europe.

The islands lie within the confines of the Madeiran National Sea Mammal Park and they are closely supervised. The success of these environmental measures can be judged by the fate of monk seals. Colonies of this endangered species are now said to be thriving on the islands.

8

WALKING ON MADEIRA

The walks described here are suited for both casual walkers and serious hikers. Walking along the *levadas* has the great advantage of giving access to the mountains along level paths, with virtually no climbing, all giving superb views. The *levada* paths are usually in good condition, sometimes quite wide but often a narrow track alongside the water channel. Some require a good head for heights.

Walking enthusiasts will know that in general it takes 10 minutes to walk 1km (0.6miles), but in the mountains allow 15, perhaps even 20 minutes per kilometre — in other words about 3km per hour. Remember about the effect of altitude and also that the terrain is often rough and the paths next to the *levadas* can be slippery, so wear strong shoes. A sun hat is also essential, waterproofs and jumpers may be required, plus a torch for some of the *levada* tunnels. To enjoy the best views, set off early. Those mountain tops that make such an attractive backdrop are often shrouded in clouds by lunchtime!

Some of the mountain peaks are easy to walk, others should be left to surefooted walkers with a good head for heights. Often the sides of the mountains drop vertically for hundreds of metres. Hardly anything grows here, just a few pitiful tree heaths. The exposed rocks at the summits contrast starkly with the lush green of the valleys.

If mists shroud the mountains, then there is a good chance that the summits will be above the clouds, but do not rely on it — the cloud layer is often too thick. So choose a cloudless day for a walk in the mountains and it will then be an unforgettable experience, but for safety do not go on your own.

Footpaths are rarely signposted so that a walker — even with a guide-book — can be faced with problems, but on the *levada* paths there is little difficulty route finding. The walking tours of Madeira organised by some travel companies are worth investigating.

1 SEA LIONS' CAVE

Reid's Hotel - Levada dos Piornais - Quebradas - Vitória - Câmara de Lobos
An easy excursion from Funchal, this varied walk along the Levada
dos Piornais offers an insight into the life of the local people. The
route skirts around banana plantations, past small traditional farmhouses, and there are few hills to climb. Even humble dwellings are
adorned with colourful displays of flowers. Most of the people here
make their living from bananas and the land is carefully tended.
During the summer season, irrigation is essential and the Levada dos
Piornais brings precious water to the outskirts of Funchal. Sluice
gates direct the water along countless smaller channels and an
ingenious process is then used to distribute it over the fields.

In the Socorridos valley, there is a magnificent view and then the
path descends into the picturesque fishing village of Câmara de
Lobos, given its name (meaning Sea Lions' Cave) by the island's
discoverers who found monk seals here. Sadly this rare and shy
species has had to seek refuge on the uninhabited Desertas Islands.
Description of walk: An easy *levada* walk with climbs and descents
of about 100m (325ft). A good head for heights is required in places.
Time: 3 hours.
How to get there and back: By town bus or taxi to Reid's Hotel.
Return to Funchal on one of the regular buses from Câmara de Lobos.
Directions: Start from the old-style Reid's Hotel, one of the most
striking hotels in Funchal's hotel quarter. At one time, this grand
hotel was as famous as London's Ritz or Singapore's Raffles. For
many visitors to Madeira, their stay is not complete without taking
tea at Reid's and strolling around the magnificent gardens.

From Reid's head towards the town along the Estrada Monumental, but after 300m take a left turn up the steep Rua do Dr Pita. Keep
left at the first junction, then take a right turn into a steep lane lined
with bougainvillea and hibiscus, the Ladeira da Casa Branca. You
will soon find yourself back on a wide road (15 minutes). After a few
metres a flight of steps leads down to the Levada dos Piornais.

The *levada* is walled with concrete and is easy to walk along. In one
or two places, there is a possibility of vertigo, but railings do provide
some protection. The banana plantations offer a quiet setting for the
walker as traffic roars along the coast road below. The Lido swimming pool can be seen at the sea's edge (25 minutes) and soon the
levada reaches the first junction. It continues in a straight line rising
a few metres as Cabo Girão looms ahead. The *levada* crosses another
road (40 minutes) and when it reaches a second wider road, it seems
to end (45 minutes) but re-emerges a few metres further up the hill.
Beneath an electricity sub-station, a wide concrete path runs along

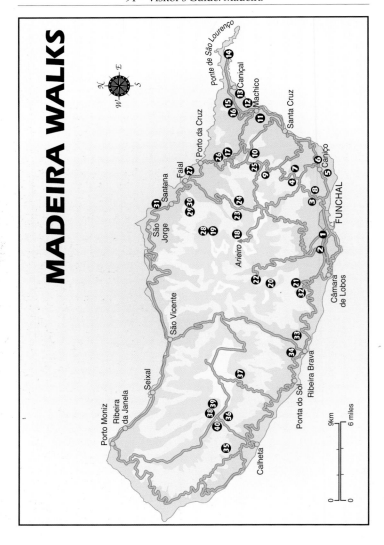

The final section of Walk 1 into the Soccoridos valley is only for those with ⇨
a head for heights, but the earlier sections are easy and give fine views

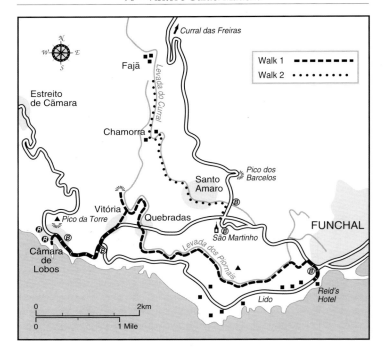

the *levada* which for the first section is covered with slabs, but this path soon becomes narrower. A steep track later crosses the *levada* (1 hour 5 minutes).

Another road crosses the *levada* (1 hour 15 minutes) and if this is followed uphill to the right, a made-up path forks off to the left. It goes to a private house, behind which a flight of steps descends to the *levada*, at this point covered with concrete slabs. After 1 hour 25 minutes, more steps climb to another road, which goes first to the right and then immediately left under a bridge by a stop sign. Continue for about 100m and then, after another stop sign, turn left down past the school at Quebradas. Proceed as far as a right-hand bend (1 hour 35 minutes) where the rushing waters of the *levada* will become audible. Beyond the bend, a few steps lead up to the *levada*.

Cross two made-up tracks and then down to the left, the Ribeira dos Socorridos valley comes into view. The *levada* leads into the valley and from this point on, there is a risk of vertigo. Leaving the cultivated land behind, make for the huge eucalyptus and acacia trees (2 hours 5 minutes) where there is a splendid view into a narrow, lush green valley. Turn round here and return to the last made-up track (2 hours 20 minutes). First the path and then a steep road lead down through the village of Vitória to the coast road (2 hours 35 minutes). A bus stop is situated close to the junction of the side road and the main road and from here there is a frequent bus service into Funchal. Either catch a bus here or follow the road into Câmara de Lobos, past a cement factory and the only oil-powered electricity generator on the island. After 2 hours 50 minutes, the first houses appear. At a petrol station, the road heads down to the left to the ugly concrete market hall. Here the road forks left to the picturesque harbour (3 hours). The splendid baroque-style church at the other end of the town is certainly worth a visit. Three fish restaurants, the 'Coral', 'Riba-Mar' and 'Os Veteranos' are recommended.

2   THE DESERTED VILLAGE OF FAJÃ

São Martinho - Levada do Curral - Santo Amaro - Chamorra - Fajã

The lower reaches of the Curral valley, or the Socorridos as it is known, are without doubt rank among the most beautiful areas of Madeira. The name, which means the valley of the 'saved', originates from the time of the island's discoverer, Zarco, and an occasion when several of his followers were almost drowned in the flooded waters of the valley. They were eventually saved with the help of a small boat. It is difficult to imagine such an occurrence these days as little water flows down the valley. Most of it is now channelled into irrigation ducts which descend the steep, often vertical rock faces. The Levada do Curral can easily be followed as far as the deserted village of Fajã and along the route, walkers will discover the magnificent views of the gorge's luxuriant vegetation.

Description: An easy *levada* walk without any appreciable gradients but a good head for heights is required in places.

Time: 3 hours for the return journey.

How to get there and back: Town bus 8 or 9 or a taxi to São Martinho.

Directions: Start at the church in São Martinho which is set on a hill to the west of Funchal and visible from some distance. The first uphill stage starts in Caminho do Esmeraldo, but you can go one stop further on the bus and the *levada* path will be directly adjacent. At this point the watercourse is covered by concrete slabs, branching off to the left between the houses opposite the bus stop sign (*Paragem*). This spot is about 500m from the church and over a bridge which crosses the four-lane Funchal by-pass.

The *levada* runs between houses and banana plantations. Where there are no slabs covering the watercourse, you can walk on a narrow but safe wall. After passing a large building-material warehouse on the right, the *levada* would appear to end by a road (25 minutes) which you should follow to the right as far as a junction. Follow a track straight on here and the *levada* re-emerges. Fields of sweet potatoes border the path and there are two smaller valleys to cross. Tiny banana plantations cling to the sides of the valleys, while the valley floor is overgrown with reeds. Dotted around the fields lie pretty houses with attractive displays of flowers. Views include Cabo Girão, the Câmara de Lobos region and later the Curral valley. Protective railings will help you over the steep sections of the path.

Ribeira do Arvoredo, a slightly bigger valley, which leads into the Curral valley, has to be negotiated. The upper part of the gorge is a jungle of eucalyptus, reeds and creepers. A bridge crosses the stream (1 hour). In winter, water drips constantly on to the path from the overhanging rocks. The *levada* joins the main valley at the hamlet of Chamorra (1 hour 10 minutes) and then beyond a right-hand bend, the path suddenly rises high above the Curral valley. There is a danger of vertigo for a few metres but after a while the *levada* turns to the left, the incline becomes less steep and bushes line the wall.

The path now continues into the delightful valley. Walls of rock on both sides alternate with stepped slopes of woodland or small terraced fields. Again there is a danger of vertigo, even though the most hazardous sections are protected with railings. Beyond a eucalyptus wood, the *levada* passes several terraced fields and a small group of houses (1 hour 30 minutes). Vines and fruit grow here, but the houses in Fajã have been deserted since the 1970s, although the fields which remain are farmed from Chamorra.

The *levada* is impassable in places from here on and towards Curral das Freiras, it becomes extremely dangerous. Ideally you should take a rest near the houses, enjoy the view and then return to Funchal. Either take the bus from the end of the *levada* or walk on to the church in São Martinho. The door into the chapel is usually locked but stop to admire the mosaic pattern on the square in front of the church.

3   PRECIOUS WATER FROM THE NORTH
Blandy's Garden - Quinto do Pomar - Romeiros - Babosas - Monte
Water supplies to Funchal and many other places on the south coast were safeguarded in 1966 by the Levada dos Tornos. The surplus water in the north of the island is collected there and then channelled through a tunnel to the hydro-electric power station in the Fajã-da-Nogueira valley (near Ribeiro Frio). It then passes through another tunnel to the south coast, emerging near Monte. The *levada* extends round as far as Santa Cruz and feeds about 100,000 outlets and provides reliable irrigation for 10,000ha (25,000 acres).

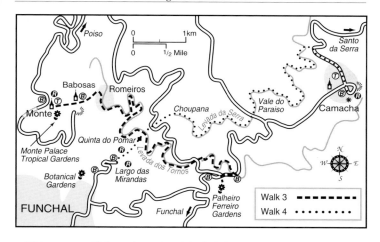

This easy walk begins in the delightful parkland belonging to the Blandy family. The Levada dos Tornos passes first through eucalyptus woods and later by houses in the village of Romeiros. A short, steep incline down into the Ribeira de João Gomes valley follows before the walk crosses to the opposite side of the valley and the viewpoint at Babosas Balcony. The walk can be continued into Monte, the nearby place of pilgrimage.

Description: An easy *levada* walk without any appreciable gradients.
Time: 2 hours.
How to get there and back: Take the 29 bus from Funchal towards Camacha and alight at the Levada dos Tornos bus stop. Buses run every hour. Alternatively, take the 77 bus to Santo da Serra and again, alight at the Levada dos Tornos bus stop. Buses leave at 8.30am (Sunday), 10.30am (Monday-Saturday) and 2pm. Return to Funchal on the 22 town bus from Largo das Babosas (leave every hour, journey time 20 minutes) or from Monte.
Directions: Start the walk from the bus stop at Levada dos Tornos, the stop after Blandy's Garden and situated at the edge of a wood on a left-hand bend. A visit to Blandy's Garden before the walk would certainly be worthwhile. This vast parkland, set out partly in the English and partly in the French style, has displays of sub-tropical plants from every country with climates similar to Madeira's. The English Blandy family are now the owners of the estate, which includes an elegant country house and the gardens are only open to the public in the mornings (Monday-Friday). Walk up the road which climbs about 500m (1,650ft) as far as the bus stop and the spot

where the Levada dos Tornos crosses the main road. Opposite the bus stop, coming from below and to the left, the *levada* leads off into the wood. The path along the *levada* is wide, passing first beneath tall eucalyptus trees. Small detached houses line the sides of the *levada*.

Cross a tarred road (25 minutes) and proceed alongside the *levada*. After some distance, a weathered sign (55 minutes) to the Quinta do Pomar blocks the path and here the *levada* flows through private land. To walk around the edge of the Quinta turn up to the right before the sign. Look for a path which runs to the left as far as a made-up road (1 hour). Follow this downhill for a short distance.

The *levada* flows behind the road between tall trees and under-neath, in the spring, you cannot miss the white, cornet-shaped flowers of the arum lily, a plant which originated in southern Africa. Just before the small village of Romeiros, you can look out over the Ribeira de João Gomes valley to Monte, a place of pilgrimage on the opposite side. Walkers should leave the *levada* behind here and proceed through the village. If in doubt, children will show you the way. After a few metres, you will rejoin the wood and a steep cobbled path leads down into the Ribeira de João Gomes valley. On the other side of the valley, the path leads up to the Babosas viewpoint (2 hours), where there is a bus stop. At the Largo das Babosas stands the chapel of Nossa Senhora de Conceição, which dates from 1906. It is usually closed. Carry straight on to Monte and visit the pilgrimage church. Also worth a visit is the unusual Monte Palace Tropical Gardens, which opened in 1991.

4 THE OLD LEVADA
Camacha - Vale do Paraíso - Choupana - Largo das Mirandas
The Levada do Serra do Faial, one time an important source of water for Funchal, has become largely redundant. Originating in the wetter northern part of the island, it skirts numerous mountain ridges and valleys with very few significant drops as far as the south-east coast. It has been superseded by the modern Levada dos Tornos, but this wide *levada* has not been allowed to fall into disrepair. The lowest section runs from the basket-weaving village of Camacha through fertile farmland and scented eucalyptus woods. It finally drops steeply towards the outskirts of Funchal. This walk can be combined with a visit to the Botanical Gardens or the bird park.

Description: An easy walk by the *levada* but with a steep descent of about 300m (1,000ft) towards the end. **Time**: about 3 hours.

How to get there and back: 29 or 77 bus from Funchal to Camacha (centre). Buses run about every hour with a journey time of 40 minutes. Return to Funchal on the 29 town bus from Largo das

Mirandas. Journey time about 25 minutes.

Directions: To reach the Levada da Serra do Faial from the central square in Camacha, also the main bus stop and a taxi rank, first follow the road past the church in the direction of Santo da Serra. Follow the signposted route up to the *levada*. A pathway carries on uphill and to the left stands a high wall overgrown with ivy, hiding the estate of the Quinta das Almas with many fine old trees. Country houses such as this were built during the last century by wealthy, predominantly English families in and around Camacha to escape the high summer temperatures in Funchal.

The path joins the Levada da Serra (20 minutes) by a small group of houses. A sign points to the left to Choupana. Primeval-looking tree ferns line the path, contrasting with the bright red roofs of the small houses. First negotiate the small valley, where willows for Camacha's basket-making industry grow. In some places a variety of cabbage, similar in some ways to Brussels sprouts, can be seen. This is shredded and used in Caldo Verde, a traditional Portuguese soup.

A signpost to 'Levada da Serra' indicating a short cut will soon appear pointing up to the right (40 minutes). Near a group of houses, it leads off to the right as far as a track and then, with a left turn, back down to the *levada* (45 minutes).

Turn right and follow the wide pathway which now runs alongside the *levada*. A flight of steps leads on to the *levada* wall and the watercourse then continues into a pine wood. From here on, gnarled oaks border the *levada*. It later runs beneath scented acacia trees, with occasional glimpses of the broad valley below. Other paths branch off to the right and left but these should be ignored. The path also crosses a road (1 hour 50 minutes). Beyond the road the *levada* passes through an area of ancient laurel woodland, which once covered nearly the whole island. The remaining examples are threatened by the Australian hedge laurel — a tree or shrub similar to the laurel. It can be identified by its orange-coloured flowers. It was originally planted as a windbreak but it has spread quickly and is replacing the native vegetation.

You will pass another country house, the Quinta Vale Paraíso (1 hour 55 minutes). Little can be seen of the house and the parkland is overgrown. The *levada* now proceeds for some distance through a damp eucalyptus wood. Horse-shoe prints bear witness to the fact that horses from the nearby riding club also use this path from time to time. Keep straight on beside the *levada* which at this point has dried up. The path soon joins a narrow track (2 hours 50 minutes), and the *levada* and track descend steeply to a tarred road. Cross the road and keep going down the pathway, passing a tree nursery the right. Shortly after, cross the Levada dos Tornos (3 hours) and then pass by the Quinta do Pomar. After another steep descent, bear left at the junction along Caminho das Voltas (3 hours 15 minutes). You will pass two small restaurants on a wide street (3 hours 30 minutes) where the Largo das Mirandas bus stop is situated.

If you visit the Botanical Gardens (open daily) on the return journey it is better to take the bus down to the gardens as the last stage of the descent is very steep.

5   MEMORIES OF RIO
Caniço - Livramento - Garajau - Ponta do Garajau

Caniço is not just the centre for Madeira's onion farmers. Vines and tropical fruit thrive in the mild climate of the coastal zone. A small, almost forgotten *levada* passes through this fertile terrain to Garajau, a coastal village away from the hurly-burly of central Funchal. Garajau has become a refuge for the well-to-do who, like the tourists, are seeking a measure of peace and quiet.

The steep cliff faces have become favourite nesting grounds for terns (garajau means 'tern' in Portuguese) and there is only room for a few coarse shingle beaches. In between, headlands jut out into the sea. On an exposed position on the Ponta da Garajau promontory stands a statue of Christ. Built in 1927, it resembles a much bigger statue in Rio de Janeiro. This spot also offers a fine view over Funchal. **Description**: An easy *levada* walk without any difficult gradients, although the path is somewhat overgrown in places. **Time**: 2 hours. **How to get there and back**: Take the number 2 bus from Funchal to Assomada and alight in Caniço town centre. Buses leave every hour and the journey takes about 30 minutes. From Machico, buses run to Funchal every hour via Caniço. Alight in Caniço town centre but be

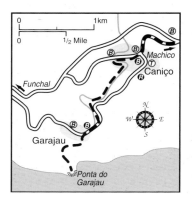

careful as the bus from Machico stops on the main road above the town centre. The journey takes about 40 minutes.

Returning from Garajau to Funchal, take the 136 bus. 12 noon (Sunday), 1.15pm (Monday-Saturday), 6pm (Monday-Saturday), 7.30pm (Sunday) or the 155 bus at 3.10pm (Monday-Saturday), 8.10pm (Monday-Saturday) with a journey time of 30 minutes. Alternatively, take a taxi or walk to Caniço town centre and then one of the hourly buses to Funchal or Machico.

Directions: The bus from Funchal stops above the church in the centre of Caniço in a square with snack bar and taxi rank. To find the *levada* to Garajau, start back uphill along the road to Funchal, past a filling station and a junction. A few metres past the bus stop, a flight of steps on the left leads down to the *levada*. The *levada* path, at the start quite wide, passes a banana plantation and a few houses, but it later narrows and in places is rather overgrown, as it is little used. The *levada* slopes almost imperceptibly downhill through orchards. Orange and avocado pear trees, pineapple and Japanese medlar plants border the path. It is here that the exotic fruit on view in Funchal's market hall are grown.

By a water basin a few steps lead down to the left (20 minutes). The *levada* continues on the right beneath the wall. It passes a few more water basins — vital in the Caniço region, the driest and sunniest in Madeira, where farmers have considerable water requirements. Exotic fruit of all kinds certainly thrive here, but constant irrigation is an essential ingredient for success. The farmers rent 'water hours', during which time they can use the water flowing from the channel.

Belladonna lilies often grow alongside levada paths

It is stored in tanks and then released on to the fields as required.

This walk offers frequent splendid views out to sea and the Desertas Islands, a string of uninhabited islands in the Madeiran archipelago. Cross a tarred road (30 minutes) and then a few metres further down, the *levada* re-emerges. Suddenly in front of you a deep valley unfolds (40 minutes) and then, just a few metres below the *levada*, the road from Caniço to Garajau comes into sight. You will appreciate the sweeping view over the sea down to Caniço de Baixo and a striking headland, known as Ponta da Atalaia. This prominent rock stands guard over the sea like a watch-tower (*atalaia* means watch-tower in Portuguese).

Past a right-hand bend, the *levada* path has been destroyed by construction work. It is therefore advisable to clamber down a beaten path to the road and to follow this to the right in the direction of Garajau. This road runs in a wide arc round the valley and soon the first houses of Garajau appear. Immediately to the right is a pleasant café which serves hot lunches. The menu changes daily.

At the junction a few metres further on (1 hour), take a left turn downhill between some new houses. At the end of the walk, the statue of Christ at Garajau can be seen clearly. Bear left at the fork (1 hour 20 minutes) and then take a path to the right. The statue is now only a short distance away (1 hour 30 minutes) and once there, you will be rewarded with a fine view. It comes as a surprise that Funchal is visible from here. There is also an attractive picnic site with tables and benches. Finally, return to Garajau via the same route (2 hours).

6 ONIONS, PAWPAWS AND IDYLLIC BEACHES
Tendeira - Zimbreiros - Reis Magos - Caniço de Baixo
Few people know about the delightful coastal path which links Tendeira, the beach at Reis Magos and Caniço de Baixo.

Description: An easy *levada* walk, although certain sections in the middle are likely to induce a little vertigo and stout shoes are essential. **Time**: 1 hour.

How to get there and back: Take one of the regular buses from Funchal or Machico along the coast road to Tendeira. Take care on the 2 bus as this route only goes as far as Assomada. Journey time from Funchal is 40 minutes. Return to Funchal from Caniço de Baixo on the 155 bus at 2.15pm, 3.00pm (Monday-Saturday), 6.15pm, 8pm (Monday-Saturday). Journey time 40 minutes. Alternatively, take a taxi to Caniço (town centre) and then on to Funchal or Machico on one of the hourly buses. (Take care as buses to Machico follow the main road above the town).

Directions: Coming into the small town of Tendeira from Funchal, beyond a bend on the left stands a bright blue house with dark blue shutters. Directly behind this house is a bus stop. On the seaward-side, a car park was created when the coast road was straightened. Above the car park, two paths branch to the left.

Take the one on the left, a made-up path. It runs downhill past an electricity sub-station to an umbrella-shaped tree (5 minutes). At this point, a *levada* crosses the path. Take the *levada* to the right across the town to a track which then carries on downhill to the right.

The path ends behind the last houses, but a beaten path runs alongside a wall. Some 20m further on, a flight of stairs descends steeply towards a tiny house with red window frames. Keep straight on past more houses until a tarred road (20 minutes) appears. Turn right along this road as it gently slopes downhill.

A partly modern, partly traditional-style farm with water basins and tiny fields, wrested from the otherwise dry barren land, breaks up the countryside. What seems like wasteland is in fact used to grow grass for cattle fodder.

First keep straight on at a junction (30 minutes) and soon after, a small valley appears. The moist, sheltered land is ideal for growing pawpaws and bananas. The tarred road ends beyond the valley (40 minutes).

First continue straight on along a field path, but this soon comes to an end high above a gorge. It is possible then to descend into the gorge, through a terraced field below the path and, at its lower edge, you will join a very narrow beaten path running parallel to the sides of the valley. At the foot of the valley, clamber over the narrow and rocky river bed (55 minutes). On the other side of the valley, climb up the side to a wider footpath, which then leads uphill in front of a wall diagonally to the left and then to a tarred track. Follow this down to the left between a few houses and soon a magnificent view will open up — to the left over the striking Ponta da Atalaia headland and the bathing complex at Reis Magos down to the right.

The beach (1 hour 10 minutes) where there is a pleasant restaurant and bar is not far now. Despite the shingle it is a popular place during the summer. The path now continues past some beach huts towards the high-

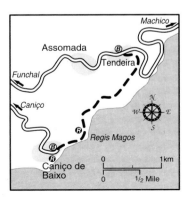

rise block in Caniço de Baixo. A very wide path crosses the Caniço river and heads up towards the splendid villas and magnificent gardens of this holiday resort. Walkers will find snack bars, restaurants and plenty of other amenities. The bus stop is nearby.

7 THROUGH THE PORTO NOVO VALLEY

Camacha - Salgados - Levada do Caniço - Assomada

The Levada do Caniço is not a 'tributary' of the modern Levada dos Tornos, but it draws its water from the Porto Novo river. The latter's source lies to the east of the central highlands and the river brings an ample supply of water to the south-east coast. This *levada* was built many years ago and the wild, almost primeval, atmosphere of the desolate Porto Novo valley is very popular with walkers. After a steep descent, the walk follows the leisurely course of the *levada* and then drops down to Assomada on the coast road.

Description: A walk of medium difficulty with a steep descent of about 300m (1,000 ft) at the beginning. **Time**: 2 hours.

How to get there and back: Take the 29 or 77 bus from Funchal to Camacha (town centre). Buses run every hour and the journey time is 40 minutes. Return on one of the frequent coast road buses to Funchal or Machico.

Directions: At the far end of Camacha's town square behind the large white basket-weaving centre known as the 'Café Relógio' and a viewing platform with a fine view over the south-east coast, stands the local health centre (Centro de Saúde). To the left a steep path leads downhill and in wet weather it can be rather slippery. Turn left

at a school (10 minutes) and then continue the very steep descent before a narrow *levada* crosses the path (20 minutes). Do not take the wide path which turns to the left and runs alongside it, but continue in the same direction on a narrow beaten path. Scattered houses, hidden away between orchards and vegetable gardens, make up the small village of Salgados and some border the path, but then you will join the Levada do Caniço (30 minutes) and the steep descent ends. A path leads straight down to the Porto Novo river but instead turn right and follow the *levada* which runs high above the river without any appreciable gradients. Lush vegetation characterises the Porto Novo valley. The man-made terracing on the steep slopes is little used today. Working in this inaccessible part of the valley is too arduous and trees have now been planted here.

The slopes are steep but the *levada* path is easily negotiated without fear of vertigo. This walk is particularly attractive in the spring when the gleaming yellow broom flowers brighten up the banks of the water channel. Continue a few metres beyond the entrance of the tunnel (1 hour 30 minutes) to a small viewing terrace and the return and pass through the short tunnel. The first house of Assomada will soon come into view (1 hour 45 minutes) but you will find the *levada* path blocked. So turn left and join a wide track. First carry straight on along this track, then turn right and wind your way downhill. Keep the church of Assomada within your sights and once you have passed round to the left of the church, you will find yourself on the main road from Machico to Funchal (2 hours). A few metres up the hill is the bus stop.

8   THE BASKET-MAKERS

Levada dos Tornos - Palheiro Ferreiro - Nogueira - Ribeirinha - Camacha
The basket-makers of Camacha can look back over a long tradition. For many years coarsely-woven baskets made with brown, 'un-cooked' cane have been used for carrying and storing produce. Last century, two English visitors with summer houses in Camacha brought with them some Italian baskets, which were copied by the skilful Madeiran craftsmen and women. Before long, the wicker-work industry had become established, producing baskets first for the British families on the island and then for export. Sometimes, whole families are involved and in fact the majority of Camacha's inhabitants are dependent on the basket-making industry. A section of the Levada dos Tornos passes through woods and fertile valleys before passing to the south of Camacha. The walk can be concluded with a tour of the basket-making workshop.

Description: An easy *levada* walk without any significant inclines.
Time: 2 hours.

How to get there and back: As for Walk 3. Return to Funchal by bus 29 or 77, both run every hour. Journey time 40 minutes.

Directions: This walk begins at the Levada dos Tornos bus stop (see Walk 3). Coming from Funchal, the *levada* path to Camacha is on the right by the bus stop sign. On the left stands a pink house with a particularly attractive garden. Continue through an acacia wood but then, below the football pitch (7 minutes), the *levada* disappears. A wide path leads to a tarred road. Follow this for a few metres to the left and you will see the *levada* re-appear on the right-hand side. It then passes a few houses and enters a wood of tall eucalyptus trees.

The *levada* curves sharply around a small valley before a low tunnel unexpectedly appears in front of you (20 minutes). It is only passable with the help of a torch and you will have to keep your head well down. Furthermore, the tunnel is very narrow and slippery. Some may prefer to take the footpath to the right, before the tunnel entrance, up to a cluster of houses where it joins a made-up track (30 minutes). Turn left and pass through the small village of Palheiro Ferreiro. After about 200m, branch off to the right into a tarred road and follow this downhill for about 150m until a concrete path turns off up to a blue-washed house. A narrow, partly made-up path runs past this house and down the slope. Before reaching the valley bottom, keep left above a thatched house. Keep left again, cross the stream and before long you are back by the Levada dos Tornos.

Turn right along the *levada* path as far as a junction where three paths meet (55 minutes). Carry straight on and in a few metres you will find yourself back by the *levada*. The watercourse now runs around the Nogueira valley with its many layers of terracing. Willows for the basket-makers as well as fruit are grown here. Pass a cluster of houses (1 hour 5 minutes) and shortly after the *levada* will again disappear into a tunnel (1 hour 20 minutes), but this one is unpassable, so proceed past the small hut on the left and climb up a steep beaten path to a wide track. Turn right across a junction to the main road from Caniço to Camacha (1 hour 30 minutes). Follow this road to the left for a short distance and after about 150m, a made-up track branches off to the right. First gently and then once past a junction more steeply it descends into the Ribeirinha valley. A white sign points the way to the Levada dos Tornos (1 hour 40 minutes).

To get to Camacha, ignore this sign but keep going uphill on the track. Bear left at a fork along a tarred road and left again at another fork (1 hour 50 minutes) a little further on. Shortly after, a wide track on the right leads up to Camacha's town square (2 hours). The bus stop and taxi rank are situated on the left but do not miss the opportunity to visit the Café Relógio basket-making centre (open weekdays) in the large white building on the right. Inside you will find salerooms, a cafeteria and a restaurant, where the famous Camacha folk dancing group often perform.

9 A GENTLE STROLL UNDER THE OAK TREES
Sitio das Quatro Estradas - Levada da Serra - Rochão - Camacha

The Levada da Serra do Faial is rarely used nowadays, but it has a special charm for the walker. For long stretches to the north of Camacha the water channel, which generally runs through dense woodland, is lined by oak trees which were planted on both sides of the channel when it was built. Now mature and gnarled, the oaks' ample foliage arches over the *levada*. It is invariably cloudy, even misty here, but the sun often breaks through and clears away the clouds and then the ground starts to steam, creating a tropical rainforest in miniature.

Description: An easy *levada* walk without any appreciable gradients.
Time: 3 hours.

How to get there and back: Take the 77 bus from Funchal to Santo da Serra as far as Sitio das Quatro Estradas at 8.30am (Sunday), 10.30am (Monday-Saturday), 2pm. Journey time 1 hour. Return to Funchal from Camacha by 29 or 77 buses which run about every hour. Journey time 40 minutes.

Description: Just beyond the small village of João Frino, the road to Poiso branches left off the main road from Camacha to Santo da Serra. At this cross-roads lies the Sitio das Quatro Estradas (Place of the Four Roads), named after a junction of four important roads — used in the twentieth century by porters carrying goods from place to place. Alight at the bus stop and proceed up the hill to Poiso and the Levada da Serra (10 minutes). On the right you will pass a pig-fattening farm, which provides Madeira with fresh meat.

At the edge of the wood, join

the *levada* path and set off to the right in the direction of Camacha. There are no perceptible inclines in the path as it makes its way past the tall eucalyptus trees and gnarled oaks which line both sides of the *levada*. Suddenly, the channel emerges from the shade into the open (1 hour 5 minutes) and there appears a commanding view over the east of the island, including the eastern tip at Ponta de São Lourenço. Now and then, a buzzard may circle high over the treetops.

Cross a track and then a path by which a narrow *levada* rushes down to the valley (1 hour 10 minutes). After a while there follows an avenue of oak trees and thick woodland until a white house with green shutters comes into view (1 hour 40 minutes). At this point, you will have to leave the *levada* and continue on a track as the *levada* disappears from view for some time. Beside some houses further on, take a right fork and then carry on into the wood. The path runs through a rocky cleft under a bridge and then into a long, deeply carved valley. At the far end of the valley, a concrete bridge crosses the wide stream (2 hours 10 minutes).

Once the valley has been negotiated, the path joins a narrow tarred road (2 hours 30 minutes). A path opposite leads downhill for a short distance and here the *levada* re-appears and then proceeds through the small town of Rochão. The *levada* rounds another valley and then links up with a wide path near a cluster of houses (2 hours 40

The agricultural landscape near Aguas Mansas

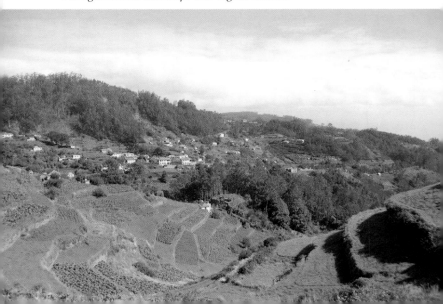

minutes). This spot is unmistakeable as a signpost indicates the route to Choupana and Faial. The path now descends into Camacha. It links up with a road which will soon bring you past the church to the central town square (3 hours).

10   COOL SUMMER DAYS IN THE TOWNS
Santo da Serra - Marco de Poiso - Massapez - Santa Cruz
Luxuriant vegetation and a climate without extremes have made Santo da Serra one of the most desirable towns on the island. During the last century it attracted wealthy business families from Funchal and they built their summer homes here, but today many do not have the money to keep them in good repair. The Madeiran middle classes now have weekend homes in the town and leisure facilities such as a golf course, tennis courts, playgrounds, picnic sites, a wild-life reserve and some fine walks have also drawn the tourists. A steep made-up path through woodland and fertile terraces links Santo da Serra with the small fishing port of Santa Cruz.

Description: A walk of medium difficulty. There is a drop of 700m (2,300ft) and the path can be slippery in wet weather. **Time**: 2 hours.
How to get there and back: Take the 77 bus from Funchal to Santo da Serra at 8.30am (Saturday), 10.30am (Monday-Saturday). Journey time 1 hour 20 minutes. Alternatively, take the 20 bus from Funchal to Santo da Serra via Machico at 7.15am and 12.40pm. Journey time 1 hour 40 minutes. Return to Funchal or Machico on one of the hourly buses which run along the coast road.

Directions: The main bus stop in Santo da Serra lies near the nineteenth-century church, which is dedicated to St Anthony. The full name, and one that is seldom heard, is Santo António da Serra. The interior of the church is really quite plain. This walk starts out in the opposite direction, along the road where the bus stop is situated. Before long you will see on the left-hand side the entrance to the Quinta do Santo da Serra. At one time this estate belonged to the Blandy family but it is now a public park and certainly worth a visit. The gardens are especially beautiful during the winter, when the camellias are in full bloom. On summer weekends it is a favourite picnic spot for Madeirans.

Just beyond the park entrance on the other side of the road and hidden away behind high walls stands the old manor house. Carry straight on towards the golf course. Magnificent gardens line both sides of this road — some are overgrown as the owners cannot afford to maintain the splendour of the last century. The Quinta do Lago is one exception (15 minutes). This fine country house is used as the golf clubhouse. About 300m beyond it, a road branches off to the left

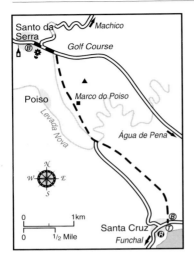

and a signpost points to the Levadas Santa Cruz. The old Quinta da Paz stands on the corner in a wild and romantic garden.

Before long, a road branches off to the right to the small village of Poiso (30 minutes), but keep left for Santa Cruz. Soon you will pass Marco do Poiso farm — unusually large by Madeiran standards — where livestock are bred on a large-scale. Before the buildings the path veers to the right and from this point descends steeply through tall trees. A fine view over the south-east coast soon begins to unfold. Many trees exhibit traces of fire damage in this region. In the early twentieth century Mediterranean maritime pines were planted here in large numbers, but during the dry summer months they are very susceptible to fire.

Continue the steep descent as far as a fork where you should bear left. This part of the walk can be quite arduous in places. Cross a *levada* (1 hour) and after passing a water basin, the first houses and fields above Santa Cruz (1 hour 10 minutes) appear. The terrain becomes a little more favourable but despite the blossoming hedges, fruit orchards and acacia groves, the descent is long and tiring. Cross a road and then pass a school. The next part of the downhill walk continues on a narrow tarred road. The fine view ahead includes the coastline, airport and the Desertas Islands. On the outskirts of Santa Cruz, the pretty houses with their tiled terraces and flower displays create an impression of prosperity.

The track now joins a wider road (1 hour 45 minutes) which continues downhill. On the right-hand side stands a small chapel with flower tubs outside. To one side is a house behind which a flight of steps leads straight down to a pathway. Use this path to get to the coast road (2 hours). On the left is a bus stop, but it is better to take the opportunity to walk through the small, well-tended park into the town centre. This is a pleasant town for a stroll and it offers several restaurants and a swimming pool.

11   THE DEVIL'S CAVES

Machico - Ribeira Grande - Furnas do Cavalum - Machico

Not far from Machico lie the Furnas do Cavalum. *Furnas* is the Portuguese word for 'caves' and *cavalum* is an old word for the 'devil'. The Devil's Caves are cut out of soft, reddish tufa rock and extend back for 30m. They can be explored in a crouched position, but only with the correct equipment and under expert guidance.

From the fifteenth to eighteenth centuries, when pirate attacks put coastal resorts at risk, Machico, a town known for its wealth derived from sugar cane, was frequently a target. If unfriendly ships were sighted, the population fled inland and hid in the Devil's Caves. In later times the caves were forgotten and, even now, they are rarely visited despite the paths which offer easy access. Only the last short stretch up to the caves involves a steep climb.

Description: An easy walk with a few short, steep inclines.

Time: 2 hours.

How to get there and back: Take the 20, 23, 53, 78, 113, or 156 bus from Funchal to Machico about every hour. Journey time 50 minutes.

Directions: Make Machico market square with its imposing parish church your starting point. Head for the bridge over the river to the old fishing quarter but, before the bridge, descend the steps to the wall which borders the river and serves as a floodwater barrier. It is easy to proceed upstream on the wall which passes the old fish-processing factory and then the closed sugar plant. About 20m behind the factory (10 minutes), the path leads down to the road.

Cross a main road (15 minutes) and a narrow track continues straight on. After about 200m turn left into a wider road and keep to the river. On Saturday many local women do their washing by the river, and chlothes are left to dry on the meadow by the river bank.

Soon the road and river separate (30 minutes). Just beyond the left turn is a small well and, at this spot, you can get down to the river bank via a narrow track and continue upstream. Turn left at a fork (35 minutes) along a road and follow this up the valley. On the right-hand side, a view over the broad and densely populated Ribeira Seca valley unfolds and this can be reached via a bridge (40 minutes). However, stay on the left bank and continue uphill on the road into a narrow valley.

Continue along this road for some distance until a bridge comes into view (1 hour). This

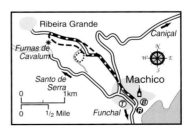

leads across the river to a cluster of houses. Beyond the bridge, several more valleys run down to the river from the right. About 100m (110yd) before the bridge, climb up a steep flight of steps to the left behind a banana field. Cross a stream and shortly after you will reach some houses. From here the walk continues to the left along a tarred track. About 100m (110yd) behind the houses on the right-hand side stands a well (1 hour 10 minutes). After a few metres a narrow path branches off to the left and leads into a large open space and, in the far right-hand corner, another steep path leads down. Follow this path for about 50m (55yd) and you will come to the Cavalum Cave (1 hour 15 minutes).

Return along the path up to the open space and follow the track to the left towards Machico. Some fine views over the bay lie ahead. This route known as the Caminho da Quinta is an old path and cobbles are visible in places under the tarred road surface. It crosses a *levada* at a sharp, left-hand bend (1 hour 25 minutes) and it is possible to make a detour to the right past some beautiful little houses with delightful displays of flowers. When you reach a steep flight of steps which crosses the *levada* (1 hour 30 minutes) take a left turn down to the road and then left again as far as a junction, which is where you would have arrived, had you not taken the *levada* detour. Follow the road downhill to Machico (2 hours).

12   BEACONS WARN OF PIRATE ATTACKS
Machico - Banda de Além - Pico de Facho

In earlier centuries Madeira was regularly a target for pirates, who attacked the rich sugar towns on the south coast. Three fortresses were built in the Bay of Machico to defend the town. On Pico de Facho (Beacon Hill, 329m/1,080ft) a look-out who sighted un-friendly ships off the coast would light a fire to warn the inhabitants. Today there is a viewpoint which offers a magnificent view over the Bay of Machico. The path to the top is steep and many visitors save themselves the effort and make the ascent by bus or taxi.

Description: A moderately difficult walk with an arduous climb and descent of about 300m (1,000ft). **Time**: 2 hours.

How to get there and back: See Walk 11

Directions: Start in the town hall square opposite Machico's parish church, where a shoeshine regularly offers his services. Cross the bridge to the eastern bank of the Machico river to the old fishing quarter of Banda de Além, which roughly translated means 'the other side of the river'. Many new businesses have opened up here and this once poor district has developed into a thriving shopping area. Take a left turn out of the large central square into a road which runs upstream parallel to the river. Soon, on the right-hand side, you will see a red-washed house (7 minutes), behind which a narrow path leads uphill between high walls. Follow this up to a higher road, turn left and continue for about 30m (35yd). Above the road you will see a large, striking building surrounded by a green, wooden fence. At the back a wide concrete path, which gradually narrows and becomes quite stony, leads uphill.

This path will take you out of the built-up area. Above the last few houses (20 minutes), you should bear right for a few metres so that you join the old path from Machico to Caniçal. It is little used nowadays and has fallen into disrepair. The low boundary walls on either side can still be seen. Initially, the path uphill is fairly straight, but it soon starts to get steeper and just above a low pylon on the left (30 minutes), the path begins to zigzag its way up the hill. The climb is really quite arduous at this point and the stony path does not help.

If you lose the path, the tall pylon on the mountain ridge serves as a helpful reference point. For the last section, the path follows a straight path to the pylon. The boundary wall is in better condition here and so it is difficult to lose your way. Suddenly you meet a tarred road (50 minutes) which was previously out of sight. It is a turning off the road to Caniçal and leads up to the viewpoint on Pico do Facho. Follow this road to the right, but make a note of where the path joins the road for when you are ready to return.

To the left there is a superb view over the Ponta da São Lourenço and soon you will see the town of Caniçal with its fishing boats bobbing up and down in the harbour. On a clear day the island of Porto Santo is visible in the distance. Walk a little further round a bend to the viewing platform. The site has been carefully laid out with picnic tables at different levels. At weekends local people come to enjoy the fine views over the bay and the valley of Machico.

Follow the same path downhill. In Banda de Além's large square there is a pleasant pavement café where you can enjoy a drink while waiting for the bus.

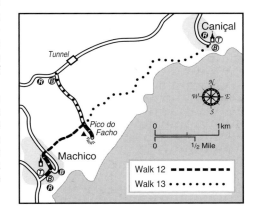

13   THE OLD COASTAL PATH

Caniçal - Ribeiro do Natal - Pico do Facho - Caniçal tunnel (western end)
It was not until the tunnel was built earlier this century that the old whaling port of Caniçal was linked with the rest of the island. Before then it was an isolated town — passengers and goods were transported to and from the rest of the island mainly by boat. A difficult road over the rocks above the coast was only wide enough to pull loads on sledges through to Machico. The path, once well-maintained and lined on both sides with boundary walls, is now only rarely used and is gradually falling into disrepair. Walkers, however, will find this one of the most attractive routes on the island.

Description: A walk of medium difficulty with a climb of 300m (325yd) on a narrow, stony path. **Time**: 2 hours.

How to get there and back: Take the 113 bus from Funchal to Caniçal via Machico at 7.30am, 8.30am (Monday-Friday), 9am, 11.15am (Monday-Saturday), 12.15pm. Journey time 1 hour 15 minutes. Return on the 113 bus from the entrance to the tunnel at 2.20pm, 5.20pm (Monday-Saturday), 6.20pm (Monday-Saturday), 7.20pm Sunday/holidays, 7.50pm (Monday-Friday).

Directions: Start from the central bus stop at Caniçal in the new square opposite the small church. Make your way back along the road to Machico, pass the church on the left and a large white building on the left as far as a small, thatched house. A flight of concrete steps leads down to the river here. Beyond the bridge, the road soon forks. Bear left along a concrete path between the houses. After a right-hand bend, you will leave the town behind you and follow a beaten path as far as a palm-lined tarred road. This road leads down to the sea. Turn right here and continue past an enclosed plantation.

The path climbs up the steeply rising coast as far as the higher end of the plantation (20 minutes). Just before a pylon, the path joins a wide track, which runs to the left through wasteland into the Ribeiro do Natal (Christmas river) valley. At the foot of the moist and sheltered valley lies a small pine wood which can be quickly crossed. Leave the path behind at the left-hand bend. Ahead is a stone bridge which crosses the stream. Directly behind the bridge the path forks. Bear left and make your way diagonally up the hillside. After a steep climb over two rocky ridges, the path up to the pylon becomes a little easier. Do not stop under the pylon, but pass above it where the path can be clearly made out. Dilapidated walls on either side mark out the path. What was once a wide footpath has now shrunk to a narrow beaten path.

From here the path leads on to a cluster of prickly pear bushes.

These cacti originated in America but they are now well established on the steep, dry slopes of the south coast. The patches of grass in between can become a carpet of wild flowers after the early spring rains. Cross a flat valley basin (45 minutes) and then continue uphill. Look back and enjoy the view over the Ponta da São Lourenço peninsula. Continue the climb up the slope of a mountain ridge and keep to the right where the path forks, continuing to follow spots of pink paint (the left hand path becomes dangerous, 50 minutes). The path leads high above the sea but suddenly, just around a bend, another valley comes into sight.

The path now descends at a comfortable pace and skirts round the valley and up a wooded mountain ridge. Hillside terraces, now only used for growing cattle feed, are visible on the left-hand side and a few cattle may be seen grazing. Continue diagonally up the slope, keeping the pylon on the next peak in sight. Cross a small acacia wood (1 hour 15 minutes) and you are at the summit with the next valley in front and the transmitting station on Pico do Facho stands opposite.

The path curves to the left on its way down the hillside to the pylon, but do not follow the narrow path on the right at a higher level. The correct path, still lined by low walls, runs several metres lower down but above the terracing. Keep heading directly towards the pylon which stands on the road to Pico do Facho (1 hour 45 minutes). From here a detour to the left up to the viewpoint on Pico do Facho is well worth the effort (see Walk 12), before continuing further along the road to the tunnel entrance (2 hours) where the bus stop is situated.

Instead of waiting for the bus at the entrance to the tunnel, walk a few metres further down the road to the 'O Tunél' restaurant, which serves coffee and home-made cakes. Give a hand signal to the bus driver immediately outside the restaurant.

14   THE SUNNY EASTERN CAPE
Ponta do Buraco - Baia de Abra - Ponta do Furado
The route to the far eastern tip of the island with its glimpses of bizarre rock formations is one of the most popular walks on Madeira. This narrow peninsula has already been badly eroded by the waves and, in places, the path crosses exposed rock, directly above the sea. It is almost certain that you will find the weather here to be dry and sunny, as the clouds simply sail over the peaks on the Ponta de São Lourenço. It rarely rains and so vegetation is sparse. Low grasses grow now where the island's discoverers found forests of dragon trees and during the early spring after the winter rains, the otherwise bleak terrain becomes a sea of colour.

Description: Initially a walk of medium difficulty on a narrow, stony path but, beyond the second viewpoint, some stretches where there is no path can be quite demanding. A sure footing and a good head for heights are required. **Time**: 3½ hours including the return journey.

How to get there and back: Take the 113 bus to Caniçal (see Walk 13). Take a taxi from Caniçal to the Baía de Abra. Arrange to return to Caniçal by taxi and then return to Funchal by the 113 bus, at 2.10pm, 5.10pm (Monday-Saturday), 6.10pm (Monday-Saturday), 7.10pm (Sunday/holidays), 7.40pm (Monday-Friday).

Directions: Follow the wide track out of the car park in Ponta do Buraco, which lies at the end of the tarred road. A beaten path soon branches off to the right. Look for the path on the opposite slope, but its precise course down into the small valley is not always easy to identify. It subsequently crosses diagonally an incline above the Baía de Abra and goes on to the northern coast of the peninsula. Bear left at the fork (15 minutes) to one of the most breathtaking viewpoints on the cape — a superb panorama over red precipices and an isolated island of lava, reshaped by the Atlantic waves.

Return to the fork and turn left to another viewing terrace (25 minutes) where the path seems to come to an end but in fact the route is marked by red paint, though in places this is often weathered and faint. The path becomes quite difficult as it involves clambering over sloping slabs and rocky ridges, but there are plenty of places to grip. You will return to the north coast at a col (35 minutes) and it will be satisfying to know that you have completed the hardest part of the walk.

Do climb the col as the impressive view from above includes volcanic rock faces worn down by the sea. The path now crosses to the southern slopes of the peninsula around a domed peak. After a few zigzags, the path leads on to another viewing terrace (55 minutes) and here the peninsula is so narrow that it is possible to look

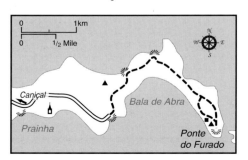

both north and south. Just before the terrace, a glance down through a narrow cleft to the left will reveal a vertical wall of rock and some 50m(160ft) below is the splashing sea.

The path now runs along a rocky ridge,

but it is probably better to clamber down and follow the easier lower path. Negotiate a small wall and then another short stretch over rocks follows. The path passes around a broad valley and in the spring, farmers from Caniçal come here with their sickles to harvest the rather meagre crop of oats, which they then feed to their cattle. Down below, the Casa da Sardinha, formerly a shepherd's hut, is now abandoned. Staying on the upper path, you will soon reach another spot where there are some splendid views along the north coast (1 hour 20 minutes). Ahead lies the tip of the peninsula, the Ponta do Furado, and reaching the top is worth the effort. The route snakes its way up a steep slope and at the end of the path (1 hour 45 minutes), a climb of a few more metres will take you to the highest point.

Take a rest and enjoy the view which encompasses the highest mountain on Madeira, the airport, the Desertas Islands and Farol Island with its distinctive lighthouse, built by a British company in the nineteenth century. On a clear day, the island of Porto Santo is also visible to the north-east.

On the return journey, you can descend to the Casa da Sardinha. A narrow path leads first to the coast and then up a slope to rejoin the main path. Follow this back to the car park, where from late morning, refreshments are usually available.

15   UNDER THE ACACIAS

Caniçal tunnel (eastern end) - Levada do Caniçal - Caniçal

It is not just the road that passes through the Caniçal tunnel, which links Machico and Caniçal, but also the Levada do Caniçal. Beyond the tunnel, it parts company with the road and the walker can follow a beaten path along the acacia-lined *levada* and enjoy the hills and uninhabited valleys north of Caniçal. Only after the tunnel was built earlier this century did water supplies reach the Ponta de São Lourenço peninsula and since then, the once parched region around Caniçal has become a centre for growing fruit and vegetables. The last part of the walk involves a steep descent into this old whaling port.

Description: An easy *levada* walk with a descent of about 250m (800ft) towards the end. **Time**: 2 hours.

How to get there and back: Take the 113 bus from Funchal to Caniçal via Machico as far as the eastern end of the tunnel. For departure times, see Walk 13. Return on the 113 bus. See Walk 14 for times.

Directions: Beyond the tunnel the Levada do Caniçal branches away from the road to the left. Keep straight on at the junction with another path (5 minutes). The *levada* goes high above the road and there is a

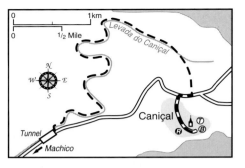

steep drop to the right — a good head for heights is required here. Beyond a bend, a fine view over Porto Santo appears and below lies Caniçal with its newly-created free trade zone in the background.

The *levada* leads round a dry valley. Below the path you can see some of the traditional, thatched huts (40 minutes) but then the path enters an acacia wood, at its best in the spring when it is a mass of yellow blossom. Heavy rainfall has carved deep furrows in the poor soil. A bridge carries the *levada* over the last section and if there is a risk of vertigo, then climb over the dried-up river bed.

Stay by the *levada* and leave the valley. The wood will soon give way to a sparse scrubland with eucalyptus trees and acacias. Pass round another small valley, but the course of this little-used path is sometimes difficult to follow so keep the *levada* in your sights. Meadows alternate with acacia groves in this totally uninhabited region.

A narrow path crosses the *levada* (1 hour 10 minutes) and beyond this point uprooted trees can make the route difficult to negotiate. The *levada* now branches off to the right (1 hour 20 minutes). A wide path, often furrowed by heavy downpours of rain, leads downhill. You will soon leave the acacia wood behind and in front of you, the Ponta de São Lourenço peninsula and the Marconi transmitting station will appear. The narrow *levada* runs to the right of the path across some wasteland. Ahead lies a small waterhouse with a wide track leading up to it. Leave the *levada* behind now as it flows on into a shallow valley. At the waterhouse the path starts to descend steeply. The first houses of Caniçal come into view (1 hour 40 minutes) and soon you will meet a road. Turn right and proceed as far as the junction into the town centre, where you should turn left to reach the main square with its church, bus stop, taxi rank, restaurants and shops (2 hours).

16 THE DANGEROUS PASS
Caniçal tunnel (western end) - Boca do Risco - Ribeira Seca - Machico
A narrow path along the steep northern coast links Porto da Cruz

and Machico. As it represented the shortest route between the two places, it was much used despite the hazards. In fact there are no difficulties to be encountered before the Boca da Risco, the 'Dangerous Pass'. Follow the Levada do Caniçal as far as the Ribeira Seca valley and then take a stony path up to the pass, from where you will be rewarded with a superb view over the north coast and the island of Porto Santo. Descend to Machico via Ribeira Seca.

Description: A walk of medium difficulty and only for the sure-footed. **Time**: 3½ hours.

How to get there and back: Take the 113 bus from Funchal to Caniçal via Machico. Alight at Pico do Facho bus stop by the western end of the tunnel. For times, see Walk 13. For return times, see Walk 11.

Directions: Before the tunnel the Levada do Caniçal branches off to the left. Follow the path under a pergola past a few houses, then the path narrows and can be rather muddy after rain. Only the acacia woods, which straddle the path here and there, have dry topsoil. Where the path traverses open countryside and small terraced fields, there are some fine views over the valley of Machico.

Ignore those paths which weave between the fields up to individual houses. The *levada* now passes deeper into the Ribeira Seca valley, the 'Dry Valley'. About 200m past a house on the left-hand side, a path climbs diagonally up and crosses the *levada* (1 hour) before the end of the valley is reached. Turn right here uphill. The turning can easily be missed, but a red dot does mark the point. Do not go beyond the *levada* junction, which is about 10m past the path

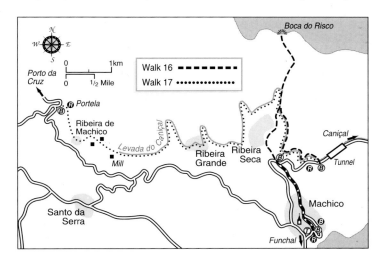

turning.

The path climbs steadily from here and parts of it are rocky, but it is nevertheless not difficult terrain. The last few terraces of the Ribeira Seca are visible on the left-hand side. Shortly after you will pass a cow byre and the path forks. Bear right and continue the climb. Open land with low scrub alternates with small pine woods. The route soon comes to resemble a mountain path. Cross two small streams, before more terraced fields and cow byres come into view. A path leads off on the right to á corrugated-iron hut (1 hour 40 minutes), but keep right and follow the red markers.

You will now pass through a broad opening in the rocks to the Boca do Risco (1 hour 45 minutes). This famous panorama affords magnificent views along the north coast to the Eagle Rock near Faial and also over to Porto Santo.

Return to the *levada* (2 hours 20 minutes), cross it and follow the path back down to the village of Ribeira Seca. Carry straight on until a flight of steps on the right branches off to a new house with strikingly large glass windows (2 hours 35 minutes). After a few metres you will reach the road and you should turn left. This leads to the main road between Machico and Caniçal (2 hours 55 minutes). Here you can wait for a bus or follow a narrow road back to Machico. It passes down through cultivated land with fruit orchards and later sugar cane plantations. At a village well (3 hours 20 minutes) turn right and then next left, which will bring you to the main square in Machico's fishing quarter of Banda de Além. To get back to the town hall square and the centre of Machico, cross the bridge on the right (3 hours 30 minutes).

17   THE LEVADA DO CANIÇAL

Portela - Ribeira de Machico - Maroços - Ribeira Seca - Caniçal tunnel (western end)

Since 1949 the Levada do Caniçal has provided the fertile valley of Machico and the barren headland of Ponta de São Lourenço with water. The precious liquid is drawn from the Red Spring (Fonte Vermelha) near Maroços and then diverted to an old mill. To get there requires what is in places a steep descent from Portela. Then the path follows the more or less level *levada* through intensively farmed land. Small terraces line the slopes and in the valley below, willows are cultivated for the basket-making industry. The path carries on through small acacia woods, which in early spring display the yellow, mimosa-like flowers so typical of the Levada do Caniçal.

Description: A walk of medium difficulty with a steep descent of 350m (1,150ft) at the beginning. **Time**: 4 hours.

How to get there and back: Take the 53 bus from Funchal to Faial via Machico, 10am (Monday-Saturday) or the 78, 8am (Sunday) to Portela. Journey time 1 hour 35 minutes. Return by the 113 bus (see Walk 13).

Directions: The bus stops outside the 'Casa da Portela' restaurant. Turn to the right of the building and then after 50m start out along a wide forest track. It leads downhill to the right into the tiny village of Ribeira de Machico with fine views over the Machico valley. You will join a road (20 minutes) in the village and should follow it to the left for about 500m where the village school is situated on the right. Just beyond, turn right along a track.

A few pretty farmhouses surrounded by terracing come into view. Before reaching the first house on the left, a path leads downhill past an annona (custard apple) tree (40 minutes). Just 15m further on before a thatched hut, turn left again and descend steeply between the fields. The route along the narrow, stony path is not straightforward. The valley floor lies at the foot and is planted with willows. The path crosses a *levada* (50 minutes) and continues downhill. Try to keep a small house with red roof tiles which lies at the foot of the valley in your sights. The path now runs almost at right angles to the slope along the edge of a terrace. Several small rivulets have to be crossed and the path can become very wet here. Several steep sections in between also have to be negotiated.

When you reach the house with the red roof (1 hour), pass to the left and follow the valley downhill. The path joins the Levada do Caniçal by a small annona plantation. Follow the *levada* and after a short distance you come on the right to a grey building — an old mill. Descend a few steps and then follow the *levada* to the left. The waterway passes several small clusters of houses which form part of the village of Maroços. Past the houses the *levada* path is wide and made of concrete, but between the fields it narrows and can become very muddy after heavy rain.

The main valley now widens and the *levada* rounds two side valleys in a wide arc. A short tunnel (1 hour 50 minutes) follows and then the path leads round in a loop into the deep Ribeira Seca valley, which is totally uninhabited. It runs alongside fields and through acacia groves, now and then a cow byre appears beside the path. Cross the Noia stream (2 hours 20 minutes), which involves descending a few steps down from the *levada* and then climbing up again on the other side.

The valley ends with the Seca stream (2 hours 55 minutes). Soon afterwards you will pass a *levada* junction and, a few metres beyond, the paths meet (3 hours). Carry straight on along the side of the *levada* until just behind a cluster of houses you reach the road between Machico and Caniçal by the tunnel entrance (4 hours). There is a bus stop nearby, but you might prefer to wait in the nearby 'O Tunél' restaurant (see Walk 13) or make a detour up the viewpoint on Pico do Facho, in which case you should follow the narrow road opposite. Allow 45 minutes for the return journey.

18 PANORAMA PATH IN THE MOUNTAINS
Pico do Arieiro - Pico das Torres - Pico Ruivo - Achada do Teixeira

The undisputed highlight of a walking holiday in Madeira is the Panorama Path from Pico do Arieiro to Pico Ruivo. It links the three highest mountains on the island — all over 1800m (6,000ft) — and is a relatively easy path to walk. In the 1960s, the tourist board transformed what was then a dangerous mountain track into a wide footpath. The first part is paved, as is the final section from the rest house on Pico Ruivo down to the Achada do Teixeira. Both routes are suitable for short walks. The Panorama Path which passes through several tunnels is protected by cables along the whole length, although heavy rainfall can cause landslips which block the path. It is always a good idea, particularly in winter, to check at the tourist office or at the *pousada* at Pico do Arieiro whether the path is safe to walk.

Description: A difficult walk at altitudes varying between 1,600 and 1,800m (5,000-6,000ft) with some steep slopes. You must be sure-

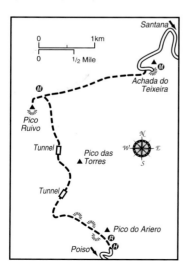

footed and have a good head for heights. A torch is recommended for the tunnels. **Time**: 3½ hours.

How to get there and back: By taxi to Pico do Arieiro. Arrange to be picked up by taxi from the Achada do Teixeira.

Directions: The road to Pico do Arieiro via Poiso is good. The welcoming bar in the modern *pousada* beneath the summit specialises in a mixer drink known as *poncho*, made from local rum, honey and lemon juice — strongly recommended in cold weather. The Panorama Path starts to the left of the bar and steps up to the summit (2 minutes) lead off to the right after just a few metres and the all-round view from the top should not be missed.

The main path continues down the steps and initially follows a rocky ridge, but it is wide and well protected. Ahead lies the end of the first stage of the walk, a small terrace with views over the north coast. Return to the main path from the terrace and, after a short climb, high, uneven steps lead down to another viewpoint (30 minutes). The drop now becomes steeper and this section is probably the hardest of the entire walk, but after these difficulties have been negotiated you will pass through a natural rock gate and shortly after, the first tunnel (50 minutes), which passes beneath Pico do Gato (1,780m/5,840ft). The tunnel is 100m long and 2m wide.

At the other end of the tunnel (55 minutes) the path forks. The old path leads off to the right around Pico das Torres. This is a dangerous route and not recommended, but anyway it is blocked off by a gate. Keep on the main path to the next tunnel, which, at 200m, is the longest on the walk (1 hour 5 minutes). It leads beneath Pico das Torres (1,851m/6,071ft), Madeira's second highest peak. The path now runs alongside an almost vertical rock face. It is here that one of Madeira's native houseleeks thrives. Shortly after you will pass through a third, short tunnel (1 hour 30 minutes). The gate at the end is left open.

On the other side of this tunnel lies another magnificent view over the north coast and to the left stands Pico Ruivo. An arduous climb through sparse heathers begins here. After another gate the path forks again (1 hour 55 minutes). Up to the left only a few metres away lies the terrace of Pico Ruivo rest house (2 hours). Enjoy a drink and a rest here before completing the last stage of the mountain walk.

The path starts on the left near the toilets and leads to a fork (2 hours 5 minutes). Carry straight on to the Encumeada pass or bear left up to the summit of Pico Ruivo (2 hours 15 minutes). The view from here encompasses almost the whole island and on a fine day it is worth lingering for a while. Return to the rest house and down to the fork beneath the building (2 hours 35 minutes). Turn left to the Achada do Teixeira. The wide, paved path offers no difficulties and the car park there is less than an hour's walk away (3 hours 30 minutes). Make a short detour to the viewpoint near the rest house at the end of the car park. It offers views of the north coast.

The start of the Panarama Path from Pico do Arieiro

19   THE HIGH ROAD FROM EAST TO WEST

Achada do Teixeira - Pico Ruivo - Torrinhas pass - Pico do Jorge - Encumeada pass.

Another fine walk follows the mountain ridge which divides the island into its northern and southern halves. Sections on the sunny southern side alternate with the shadows of the northern slopes. After the steep climb from the Achada do Teixeira to Pico Ruivo the path goes up and down past a number of peaks until it finally descends steeply to the Encumeada pass. Enjoy the magnificent views down into the valleys on either side and over the mountain ranges opposite. In early summer alpine flowers brighten the sides of the path.

Description: A demanding walk with several inclines at an altitude ranging from 1,000 to 1,800m (3,500 to 6,000ft). You must be sure-footed and have a good head for heights. **Time**: 5½ hours.

How to get there and back: Take the 133 bus from Funchal to Boaventura as far as Santana at 7am. Journey time 2 hours 15 minutes. Take a taxi from Santana to the Achada do Teixeira. Return to Funchal on bus 6 from the Encumeada pass at 3.45pm. Journey time 2 hours.

Directions: The path to Pico Ruivo forks off to the right of the Achada do Teixeira car park. First cross a meadow and then after 100m (110yd) join a wide, paved path. Initially the path is steep but later becomes easier, passing a number of small shelters. There is a fine view to the right over the north coast and to the left is Pico do Arieiro. You will soon see ahead Pico Ruivo and the rest house to the right just beneath the summit. Pass a small gate (40 minutes) and then make the short steep climb to the rest house (45 minutes).

Keep going uphill past the toilets and a little further on is a fork (50 minutes). If you have not already done so then a short detour to the summit of Pico Ruivo is thoroughly recommended (see Walk 18). Otherwise take the right fork and after a few metres you will come to a signpost indicating the Encumeada pass. The made-up path ends here and you will find yourself descending through tree heath bushes along a stony path. Pass through a gate (1 hour) and soon a narrow path will branch off to the left. Ignore this path and carry straight on following the blue markings.

The fine view down to the left is of the Curral valley. The slope is steep, but there is no risk of vertigo as bushes line the path. Parallel to the slope rises the summit of Pico do Coelho or Rabbit Mountain. To the left the range which includes the island's three highest peaks is vis-

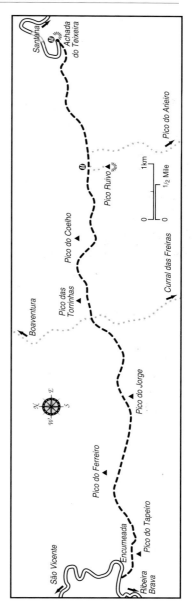

ible. Pass another gate (1 hour 35 minutes) and then beyond comes a short, steep climb. In the meantime a proper wood of huge tree heaths borders the path. Bilberry and broom can also be seen here. The path snakes up and down with bizarre rock formations on both right and left. Stones lie on the path and there is a risk of falling rocks.

At a fork (2 hours 5 minutes), the blue- and red-marked paths divide. A blue arrow indicates the way to the Curral das Freiras but you should follow the red markers to the right. The path takes a route to the north of the mountain ridge where steep, but generally safe steps lead along a rock face. The path soon becomes easier and the whole of the Curral valley comes into view.

A few weathered signposts show the way to the Torrinhas pass (2 hours) and on the right a steep path turns off to Boaventura, while the route on the left leads down to the Curral das Freiras. Carry straight on for the Encumeada pass. A steep climb is followed by a broken gate and a rock gate (2 hours 50 minutes). The view from the mountain ridge encompasses both the north and south coast, while ahead lies the Paúl da Serra. Below and to the right is the valley of São Vicente. Steps lead down directly on to Pico do Ferreiro. Clamber over a rock wall (3 hours 40 minutes) and at the next rock wall you will have to negotiate a gate (4 hours 10 minutes). The path now runs beneath a steep rock face.

Beyond another gate the path leads round a bend and then descends steeply. The summit of the smaller Pico do Tapeiro lies ahead. Pass through another gate (4 hours 50 minutes) and then a flight of steps in the rock leads up to a col. The Encumeada pass is now close by. Steps which can be slippery lead steeply downhill and there is a risk of vertigo here even though the steps are quite wide.

Soon you will reach a wide track (5 hours 25 minutes) followed shortly after by the north-south road (5 hours 30 minutes). Do not omit a short detour to the large viewing platform, a popular destination for island coach tours. Follow the road to the left where only a few metres away is a small bar and also a bus stop.

20   OLD PILGRIM ROUTE TO THE NORTH

Boca da Corrida - Boca do Cerro - Ribeira do Poço - Encumeada (or Vinháticos)

Until the end of the last century, all passengers and goods moving between Funchal and the outlying areas on the north-west coast used either boats or the mountain path between Estreito de Câmara and São Vicente. The pilgrims who made the journey every September to the religious festival in Ponta Delgado on the north coast also used this overland route. The path between Boca da Corrida and the

Encumeada pass ranks as one of the prettiest on the island. There are no appreciable variations in altitude and the pathway, which is wide and straightforward, passes through an impressive mountain landscape with fine views.

Description: A demanding mountain walk without any appreciable differences in altitude, but it should only be undertaken by surefooted walkers with a good head for heights. There are sections of the walk where prickly gorse bushes and brambles can hamper progress in places, so long trousers and a long-sleeved shirt are recommended. **Time**: 4½ hours (5 hours to Vinháticos).

How to get there and back: Take the 96 bus from Funchal to Corticeiras from 7am (Monday-Saturday), 7.05am (Sunday), 8.05am, 9.15am (Sunday). Journey time 1 hour. On foot from Corticeiras (steep climb for about 1½ hour) or by taxi to Boca da Corrida. Return to Funchal on bus 6 from Encumeada (3.45pm) or Vinháticos (4pm).

Directions: The steep, narrow, made-up road ends at the forest lodge in Boca da Corrida. A paved path leads from the car park uphill to a viewpoint where there is a splendid panorama over Curral das Freiras deep in the valley below. About 50m further, turn right on to

a field path with both Curral das Freiras and Encumeada signposted. To begin with, the slope is quite steep, but it soon becomes a little easier. The drop to the right into the valley is very steep but there is no risk of vertigo. Look back to see Funchal and its port complex and, towering in front on the opposite side of the Curral valley, rise the island's highest peaks.

Suddenly a view to the left reveals the Ribeira Brava valley, the village of Serra da Água and the Encumeada pass (20 minutes). Soon a narrow path forks off to the left (30 minutes) and a signpost indicates a route to Serra da Água, but this is an extremely dangerous path. Carry straight on along the wide path which in some places can be partially blocked by landslides. Sheep and goats graze on the meagre land while the sheltered valleys are planted with chestnut trees.

Pass through a gate (1 hour 10 minutes) and follow the path up to a col, the Boca do Cerro. Low-growing broom flowers here early in the year. On the col itself, a path signposted to Curral das Freiras forks off to the right (1 hour 20 minutes), but carry straight on towards a steep rock face, dominated behind by Pico Grande (1,654m/5,425ft). Beneath the rock face, the path turns to the left and, after a spell of wet weather, especially in the winter, the path can become very boggy. However, unusual plants such as watercress, mint and other herbs often thrive in the wet areas. Falling rocks can sometimes partially block the path. To the left there is a steep slope, making this particular stretch sometimes difficult to negotiate.

Gently, almost imperceptibly, the path descends partly through thick heather and broom, partly through huge, gnarled laurel trees. The path now winds steeply downhill and round a bend into the broad Ribeira do Poço valley. Surprisingly, at the far end of the valley, terraced fields and thatched cow byres can be seen (3 hours 10 minutes). Soon you will cross a stream and make your way out of the valley.

Before long, you will reach the water pipe which feeds the power station at Serra da Água (4 hours) and, just beyond, you join the wide track leading to the Ribeira Brava-São Vicente road (4 hours 15 minutes). Follow this main road uphill to the Encumeada pass (4 hours 30 minutes) where you will find the bus stop and, on the right-hand side, a small bar. If you have time to spare you may prefer to walk down to the Pousada dos Vinháticos (5 hours) and wait for the bus on the terrace of this elegant restaurant.

21 INTO THE NUNS' VALLEY

Corticeiras - Quinta Mis Muchachos - Boca dos Namorados - Pico do Cedro - Curral de Baixo - Curral das Freiras

In 1566 French pirates attacked Funchal and many of the townsfolk were massacred. The nuns at the Santa Clara convent, however, fled inland to Curral das Freiras to land owned by the convent. Here they were safe from persecution, as only a difficult path runs from Corticeiras over the Boca dos Namorados mountain ridge into Nuns' Valley. This path over the mountains remains an arduous trek. The first part over the pass and then steeply down in zigzags into the Curral valley is used only by walkers and forestry workers. The latter section of the walk passes through the village of Curral de Baixo, which is still without any proper road links and whose inhabitants have to bring in on foot every-thing that they do not cultivate themselves. The walk ends with a steep haul up 1,200 steps to the centre of Curral das Freiras.

Description: A demanding walk with some appreciable slopes each of about 600m (2,000ft). Only for sure-footed walkers. **Time**: 4 hours.

How to get there and back: Take the 96 bus from Funchal to Corticeiras, which runs every hour. Journey time 1 hour. Alter-natively, take a taxi to Quinta Mis Muchachos near Corti-ceiras. Return to Funchal on the 81 bus from Curral das Freiras at 12.15pm, 2.30pm (Monday-Friday), 5.45pm, 8.30pm. Journey time 1 hour 15 minutes.

Directions: Walk back some way from the terminus of the 96 bus route in Corticeiras and take the second turning on the left, a narrow made-up path. Keep going uphill to the end of the path by a farmhouse (15 minutes). If you take a taxi to Corticeiras you can start the walk here and save yourself the climb. A path now leads steeply uphill. Do not be misled by the clearings and tracks used by the forestry workers but keep to the path which soon starts to turn to the right. The last section is particularly steep and if there has been any recent rain then it can very slippery.

When you reach the Boca dos Namorados pass (Lovers' Pass; 45min), turn left and then a few metres further on, take a narrow path to the right, leading down into the Curral valley. The tall treetops soon clear with views over the Curral stream flowing in the narrow valley below, and also beyond to your destination. The slippery path now leads diagonally downhill through loose scree to the tall pylon (1 hour 5 minutes) on the rocky tip of Pico do Cedro.

The path now becomes even steeper, snaking down through sparse laurel bushes and chestnuts to a ledge (1 hour 40 minutes) where you can have rest under the shade of the trees. Carry straight on downhill. The path is now made-up again and there are a number of low steps down to a stream (2 hours 15 minutes) where the local women will often be seen doing their washing. After crossing the valley the path enters the village of Curral de Baixo (2 hours 20 minutes). Bear left at the fork. The path through the village is well maintained and much used, as there are no road links. All goods must be carried on the head or on the back.

Pass the prettily decorated houses and the small, terraced fields where a variety of fruit is grown. Cross a bridge and then soon after a flight of steps leads uphill past a school (2 hours 50 minutes). Soon you will reach the new road which has to some extent replaced the old footpath. Carry straight on for about 100m and where the road bends to the right you will find a flight of steps up the hillside. This is the beginning of an energy-sapping climb.

For a short distance, the path leads gently downhill into the foot of the Curral valley, but then, after a bridge (3 hours 30 minutes), the most demanding stretch follows. About 1,200 steps must be climbed until at last some concrete steps come into view. Before you realise it you are standing in Curral das Freiras (3 hours 55 minutes). To the left of the steps is a small bar and then a few metres further up the street lies the village square (4 hours) with the bus stop, taxi rank and several bars and restaurants. The village is famed for its chestnuts and the Nuns' Valley restaurant offers specialities made from the nuts, including soup, cakes and a liqueur.

You can miss out this last, exhausting part of the walk by carrying on along the road. It crosses the Curral stream and will take you to the 81 bus terminus.

22   THROUGH THE CRATER

Curral das Freiras - Ribeira do Cidrão - Fajã dos Cardos - Ribeira do Furado
While the lower part of the Curral stream flows through an extremely narrow gorge it comes as a surprise when the valley opens out into a hollow, which for many years was thought to be a volcano crater as it is surrounded by steep mountain sides. In fact the 'crater' was formed by erosion — the soft tufa rock near Curral das Freiras yielded more easily to the river water; in the lower reaches the flowing water could only carve a narrow passage though the hard rock. The settlement continues up the valley beyond Curral das Freiras and where the path meets the tree line there are some magnificent views over the surrounding mountain region.

Description: Medium difficulty walk with a few short, steep inclines. **Time**: 3 hours including the return journey.

How to get there and back: Take the 81 bus from Funchal to Curral das Freiras at 7.45am (Sunday-Friday), 11am, 1.15pm (Monday-Friday). Journey time 1 hour 15 minutes. For the return journey see Walk 21.

Directions: The bus goes as far as the main square in Curral das

Freiras and you should walk back a short distance along the same road. About 60m behind an electricity sub-station a side road branches off to the left (5 minutes). Follow this road to the end (15 minutes). A made-up path continues straight on and then a flight of steps leads uphill. The last few houses are now behind you and the steps climb between the fields.

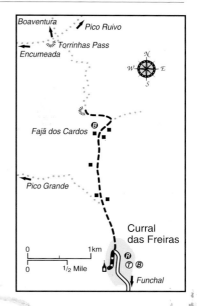

Once you have negotiated the steps (25 minutes) the path crosses a mountain stream which cascades down into the Curral valley from the mountain ridge. Behind a bridge, a path turns into a side valley but you should follow the inhabited valley north. Bear right at the fork (30 minutes) along the upper path and keep to the slope above the fast-flowing Curral stream. Willows for the basket-making industry in Camacha grow in the wet valley. The path gets nearer to the foot of the valley, but keep straight on and do not cross the stream yet. A waterfall (50 minutes) tumbles into the valley from the right. Pass a few houses and the village of Fajã dos Cardos lies some 700m (2,300ft) above. Given the sheltered south-facing position of the valley, it is possible to grow grapes here, together with oranges and other fruit. Keep straight on and do not be led astray by the sometimes quite wide paths at each side which lead to private houses. Keep a strikingly painted and tiled house in your sights. The path passes it to the right and then, just beyond, you will see on the left-hand side a bridge (1 hour 5 minutes) which crosses the stream. On the other side of the valley a path zigzags its way up the slope past tiny terraces. Slowly a magnificent panoramic view of the island's highest mountain, Pico Ruivo (1,861m/6,100ft), opens up in front.

At the fork (1 hour 20 minutes) keep left - the right-hand path just leads into the fields — and carry on to a viewpoint and, a little further on, a rainfall recording station. Cross a *levada* (1 hour 30 minutes) and you will soon reach the edge of the wood, a splendid picnic site. To the left there is a fine view down over the Curral das Freiras. Perhaps clouds are gathering in the background but they will quickly be dispersed by the mountain peaks which shelter the sun-drenched valley.

Down below flows the Ribeira do Furado and opposite you will notice some bizarre rock formations. Narrow basalt ridges emerge vertically out of the hillside. Earthquakes once opened up crevasses here, which were then filled by molten lava. The lava was harder than the surrounding rock and over millions of years the forces of erosion have left the lava exposed.

Return to Curral das Freiras by the same route. On the right-hand side of the road in Fajã dos Cardos is a small bar and shop and Curral das Freiras has more shops and bars which will probably be open.

23   A VIEWING PLATFORM HIGH ABOVE THE VALLEY
Ribeiro Frio - Balcões - Ribeiro Frio

This gentle stroll follows the Levada do Furado from Ribeiro Frio to the viewing platform at Balcões high above the Metade valley. On a clear day you can see Madeira's main mountain range and look down over the north coast, where the Eagle Rock dominates the landscape.

The trout farm at Ribeiro Frio is certainly worth a visit and at 'Victor's Bar' restaurant nearby the fish taste delicious whether grilled or freshly smoked. In the adjoining nature reserve all of Madeira's native flora are displayed and labelled.

Description: An easy *levada* stroll with hardly any inclines.

Time: 1 hour including return journey.

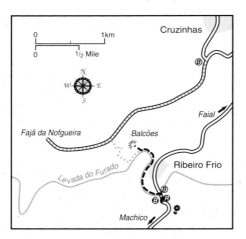

How to get there and back: Take the 103 bus from Funchal to Boaventura as far as Ribeiro Frio at 7am, 1.30pm (Monday-Saturday). Journey time 1 hour 15 minutes. Return to Funchal on the 103 bus at 2.30pm (Monday-Saturday), 6.30pm.

Directions: The bus stops below the trout farm in Ribeiro Frio outside 'Victor's Bar' restaurant. Follow the road downhill a little until you see a sign indicating the turning to Balcões (5 minutes). Follow the leisurely course of the Levada do Furado as it winds its way between the tall trees to an opening (25 minutes) cut out of the rock. There is a fork in the path just beyond. Leave the *levada* and follow the path to the right.

The viewing platform at Balcões (30 minutes) is only a few metres away and it affords a splendid view of the island's highest peaks. These are from left to right: Pico do Arieiro (1,818m/5,963ft), the jagged Pico das Torres (1,851m/6,071ft) and the rounded Pico Ruivo (1,861m/6,100ft). The Metade river flows beneath, its water feeding the power station at Fajã de Nogueira before it is diverted through a 1 km (⅔ mile) long tunnel into the Levada dos Tornos and round to the south coast.

You may like to follow the Levada do Furado a little further to the west. However, the path is often blocked by landslides. Just beyond the fork to the Balcões another path leads away from the *levada* to the right and then winds its way down to the river with one short section descending 300m (950ft). In the valley you can either take the left-hand track to the power station or turn right to the village of Cruzinhas where the bus stops.

Madeira's highest peaks: Pico do Arieiro, Pico da Torres and Rico Ruivo seen from Ribeira Frio

24 DENSE LAUREL WOODS ON THE NORTHERN SLOPES
Ribeiro Frio - Lamaceiros waterhouse - Portela

At one time dense laurel forests covered large parts of the island and in the inaccessible north they have remained untouched to this day. Upper sections of the Levada do Furado cross one of the island's largest areas of forest, now a nature reserve. The pleasant walk alongside the *levada* is interrupted by sections which require a good head for heights, but these are offset by magnificent views over the north coast. Finally the walk descends into Portela where you can enjoy an *espetada* speciality at the 'Casa da Portela' restaurant.

Description: Medium to difficult walk but without any appreciable gradients. Only for surefooted walkers with a good head for heights.

Time: 3 hours.

How to get there and back: Take the 103 bus from Funchal to Boaventura as far as Ribeiro Frio at 7am. Journey time 1 hour 15 minutes. Return on the 53 bus from Portela to Funchal via Machico at 3.45pm (Monday-Saturday), 5.15pm. Journey time 2 hours.

Directions: The path to Portela begins at 'Victor's Bar' restaurant, a timber house with rustic-style tables and benches, on the right-hand side of the road. A sign indicates a few steps down, then a small bridge leads across the stream. From here, follow the generally flat Levada do Furado on a wide, mossy path. Dense woodland with laurels and tree heaths border the *levada*. In summer the hydrangeas are in bloom and in early spring you will discover countless wild

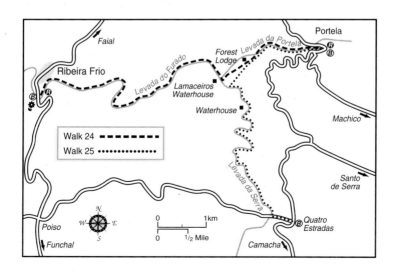

flowers. The path narrows in places and it is necessary to walk along a wall made from slippery basalt, but whenever the left side of the *levada* drops steeply the path is protected by railings.

There are many views over the gorge, and water drips and bubbles out of the rock walls. A tributary feeds into the *levada* from the right (1 hour) and, shortly after, a bridge crosses the stream. Beyond here parts of the *levada* wall can be very slippery when wet, so care must be taken. The path enters a valley and at the far end a difficult section has to be bypassed. About 20m before the end of the valley (1 hour 15 minutes) you will have to make your way down a beaten path to the bed of the stream and then up the other side. After the next bend you will have to leave the *levada* wall again for a few metres.

Another valley (1 hour 25 minutes) has to be crossed in a similar manner. You will soon catch the first glimpse of the north coast, Faial and the impressive Eagle Rock. The *levada* now passes through narrow rock openings and stone slabs or wooden beams have been laid over the channel. Another valley has to be crossed by a path (1 hour 50 minutes). There follows a difficult section which needs a detour of about 20m. Another valley is bypassed with a path.

The *levada* now flows into a tunnel about 30m in length. Carry straight on from here, but the next section does require a good head for heights. To compensate, however, there are some fine views out to the north coast and down over the coastal village of Porto da Cruz. At some points, the rocks lean so far over the *levada* that walkers have to duck. There are more tunnels to pass through, although before reaching the Lamaceiros waterhouse (2 hours 50 minutes), the path does becomes a little easier.

About 30m beyond the house after the next bend, the path to Portela (signposted) branches off. The narrow, fast-flowing *levada* runs downhill as far as the Lamaceiros forest lodge (2 hours 55 minutes) where you will join a wide track. Keep straight on perhaps resting first at the attractive picnic site. Bear left at the next fork (3 hours) and a little further on, there is a viewpoint overlooking the Eagle Rock. The path turns to the right here and leads downhill to a left turning (3 hours 5 minutes), signposted to Portela. The path which is now narrower passes between some meadows alongside a small *levada*. At a junction this curves round to the right (3 hours 10 minutes). Keep straight on beside the *levada* which runs gently downhill as far as a ruined house (3 hours 20 minutes), where a flight of steps leads steeply down to a road (3 hours 25 minutes). Turn left and follow the road for a short distance as far as the Portela pass (3 hours 30 minutes). Stop here and sample some Madeiran specialities at the friendly 'Casa da Portela' restaurant. The bus stop is nearby.

Walking beside the Levada do Furado from Ribeira Frio

25   EUCALYPTUS TREES AND HYDRANGEAS

Sitio das Quatro Estradas - Levada da Serra - Levada da Portela - Portela

Woods of tall eucalyptus trees dominate the first section of this walk. You will be able to smell the intense aroma of the oils wafting down from the leaves. The path later passes through more colourful terrain — hydrangeas border the *levada*, their round, blue flowers enlivening the summer landscape. Then you reach the north coast where a change in the weather may occur — for better or for worse. The walk ends with a steep but short descent into Portela.

Description: A *levada* walk of medium difficulty with a descent of 200m (650ft). Danger of sliding on wet clay. **Time**: 3 hours.

How to get there and back: See Walk 9. See Walk 24 for the return journey.

Directions: To reach the Levada da Serra do Faial, follow the directions given at the start of Walk 9. At the edge of the wood turn right along the wide *levada* path. Initially there is an unrestricted view over the resort of Santo da Serra and the pointed roofs of the state-run holiday complex in the foreground. Soon the path passes under the tall eucalyptus trees and follows the meandering *levada* for some distance. Dangling lichen and dense ferns, even on the trees, bear witness to the permanently damp atmosphere.

A wide track crosses the *levada* (1 hour 30 minutes) which continues straight ahead. Hedges of heather, some as tall as trees, line the path together with the hydrangeas, whose round, blue flowerheads create a particularly attractive backdrop in the summer. The large fruit on the Madeiran bilberry bushes are hard to resist.

An avenue of gnarled oaks overgrown with lichen leads to a waterhouse (1 hour 45 minutes), which is surrounded by a pretty garden. A signposted path marks the route to Santo da Serra, but the way to Portela is straight on. You will soon reach a spot where the *levada* wall is in poor condition for a distance of 50m. It is passable, but you will probably find it easier to bypass this section by using the lower path. Soon the path seems to fork, but follow the *levada* to the left. After further bends you will join a wide forest track (2 hours 15 minutes). This is where you part company with the *levada* and should proceed to the right down to a forest lodge (2 hours 25 minutes). The path passes by the lodge. From here follow the last section of Walk 24 into Portela, half hour's walk.

26   THE OLD WINE ROUTE

Portela - Cruz da Guarda - Porta da Cruz

An ancient path used to link the towns of Santo da Serra and Porto da Cruz. The famous wine from Porto da Cruz was carried along this route to Funchal in goat skins or 'borrachos'. The path leads from the Portela pass steeply down into Cruz da Guarda, alongside the Levada do Castelejo for a while and finally down into the centre of Porto da Cruz. There are many fine views over the north coast, which is dominated by the Eagle Rock. In Porto da Cruz the old mansions and also the small cemetery are particularly interesting. If you have time, pay a visit to the popular 'Penha d'Ave' café at the end of your walk.

Description: A walk of medium difficulty with a descent of 600m (2,000ft) with some sections of slippery paved path. **Time**: 2 hours.

How to get there and back: Take the 53 bus from Funchal to Faial via Machico as far as Portela, leaving Funchal at 10am (Monday-Saturday), 1pm (Monday-Saturday) or the 78 bus at 8am (Sunday), 12.30pm (holidays). Journey time 1 hour 30 minutes. Return to Funchal from Porto da Cruz on the 53 bus at 1.10pm (Sunday), 3.40pm ((Monday-Saturday), 4.55pm (Monday-Saturday) or the 78 bus at 5.40pm (Sunday). Journey time 1 hour 40 minutes.

Directions: A tarred track runs off the road to the left beside the 'Casa da Portela' restaurant but this surface soon ends. About 200m behind the restaurant a made-up path turns off the mud track. Cruz da Guarda is signposted. The path starts with a steep downhill slope and after rain the steps can be slippery, so take care.

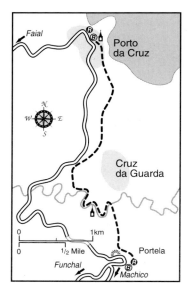

Once the pine forest has ended, cow sheds and then a few houses appear (35 minutes). This is the edge of Cruz da Guarda and before long the path forks. Bear left along a paved path and through a built-up area. A few steps lead down to the street (40 minutes), which you should follow downhill to the right for a few metres. Continue along this road which bends round to the right and then turn left into the narrow *levada* path which runs below the bend. A little higher up on the bend, another *levada* path turns off but it is a cul-de-sac.

The *levada* leads round a small valley where vegetables alternate with acacia bushes. You will then reach a road bridge and the *levada* will disappear underneath (55 minutes). About 20m before the bridge, a steep beaten path turns left up to a small electricity sub-station. Turn right towards the road over the bridge and, just beyond it, another beaten path on the right returns to the *levada*. The gorge is overrun with shrubs but, in between, you will catch sight of small sugar cane fields or plantations of the tall silver banana, a variety which is susceptible to strong winds.

About 100m beyond the bridge do not take the path to the right towards a thatched house, but keep left along the *levada* path. You will then come to a *levada* bridge (1 hour) where you should take care. The water channel is covered with concrete slabs, but there are large gaps between them. Keep on walking below the road and on a rocky ledge ahead, you will see the pretty chapel of St John Nepomuk with its double bell tower. It was built in 1776 by the aristocratic Leais family, who owned a quinta here.

A made-up path crosses the *levada* (1 hour 10 minutes). Follow this path downhill to the right and then across a thickly wooded valley. It joins a road at a bend on the opposite side (1 hour 25 minutes). Follow the road downhill for a short distance until after about 200m a cul-de-sac turns up to the right. This passes gently uphill between houses and over a small hill, behind which a stone path leads down to the coast.

At a fork (1 hour 50 minutes) follow the path to the left as it descends steeply between the vineyards and vegetable fields into the centre of Porto da Cruz. Soon you will see the town's football pitch and it is not far now to the road (1 hour 55 minutes) which leads across a bridge to the church square. You will pass the cemetery, where the crosses above the grave display pictures of the deceased. Behind the church square you will find the 'Penha d'Ave' restaurant, well-known in the area for its wide range of tropical fruit. The bus stop is in the main street, just up the hill from the church.

27 THE EAGLE ROCK

Penha da Águia de Baixo - Penha da Águia - Banda dos Moinhos

The Penha de Águia or Eagle Rock holds a special charm for those who come to admire it. This unusually shaped mass of rock rises some 590m (1,935ft) above the fertile coastal landscape between Faial and Porto da Cruz. At first sight it looks almost inaccessible, but a number of steep paths lead up to the top — the easiest route is from the western village of Penha de Águia de Baixo. This path rises steeply between terraced fields as far as a seaward-sloping plateau. It then leads through thick bush along a ridge to the summit, from where you can enjoy a magnificent panorama over the central highlands and along the coast.

Description: A strenuous walk with a climb and descent of 500m (1,640ft) along narrow, often overgrown paths. Only for sure-footed walkers with a good sense of direction. **Time**: 3 hours.

How to get there and back: Take the 103 bus from Funchal to Faial at 7am. Journey time 1 hour 45 minutes. Alternatively, take the 53 bus (via Machico) at 8am (Sunday). Then go by taxi from Faial to Penha da Águia de Baixo. Return to Funchal from Banda dos Moinhos via Machico on bus 53 at 1.05pm (Sunday), 3.35pm (Monday-Saturday), 4.50pm (Monday-Saturday) or the 78 bus at 5.35pm (Sunday).

Directions: The walk starts at the 'Galé' bar in Penha da Águia de Baixo. On the road to the right of the bar stands a pylon and to its right, a narrow beaten path leads uphill. First it passes a low concrete building and then runs steeply uphill between stone walls which mark out the small fields. Above a cow shed, the path bends across to the left and runs, not quite so steeply, alongside a wall. To the left is a fine view over Faial with its attractive church.

Beyond the wall you should keep to the left and climb over a series of rocks. The path now snakes its way up. The terraced fields are replaced by tree heath and bramble undergrowth. Climb over some more rocks and at a sloping rock wall (15 minutes) you must climb to the left to return to the beaten path. Abandoned terraces hark back to a time when wheat was cultivated on these almost inaccessible slopes. Nowadays no one is prepared to put in the backbreaking work to harvest this crop.

The path passes to the left of another rock face (20 minutes) and then continues to wind its way upwards, but it is not always easy to follow. If in doubt you should head for the cut between the two rocky ledges at the top of the incline. The path now suddenly becomes wider and flatter as it passes through low-growing tree heath above a steep drop down to the sea (30 minutes) but at least it is easy to follow here. Down below to the left the surf is blown by the north wind and you will be able to see a small beach covered with coarse scree. The path now leads up past a cluster of pines and then it becomes steeper through dense shrub. Tree-trunks are dragged along the path here and, as a result, it has become very smooth. On the left is a hollow which ends high above the coast. A small stream, not visible from above, tumbles 300m (1,000ft) down the side of the rock into the sea.

Bear left at a fork (40 minutes) but at the next junction turn right and continue up the steep slope to the rocky ridge. The course of the path disappears completely just below some rocks, but keep going uphill and you will retrieve it just below the ridge. It now leads to the left up to the ridge. On the crest the path continues uphill and on the right-hand side a rock face drops steeply into the Ribeira de São Roque valley with views over Faial and Cruzinhas (1 hour 5 minutes). Almost totally overgrown sections of path alternate with clear stretches, offering new vistas over the southern side of the island. Uprooted trees can sometimes block the path, but overcoming such obstacles is well worth the effort. The summit is now visible ahead and after a short, steep climb, a concrete column marks the highest point on the Eagle Rock (1 hour 30 minutes). From here walkers have a splendid view over the island.

Return to the 'Galé' bar for a rest and refreshments, then turn left and continue uphill to the end of the road. Beyond the turning point a narrow path runs to the left to a house with red windows. A wider path passes to the right of the house (1 hour 55 minutes) and then down to the right to the small settlement of Banda dos Moinhos on the main road from Faial to Porto da Cruz (3 hours) where there is a bus stop.

28 A STEEP PATH IN THE NORTH

Achada do Teixeira - Queimadas - Pico das Pedras (forest lodge)

The slopes on the northern side of the central highlands are steep and only in recent years has a road been built from Santana through to the Achada do Teixeira, enabling an easier ascent of Pico Ruivo. In the opposite direction a steep footpath, once the only link with the highest peak on the island, runs through thick tree heath bushes and down through the state-owned Queimadas holiday complex with its extremely attractive rhododendron parkland, duck ponds and thatched houses. From here, a secluded *levada* follows a leisurely route on to Pico das Pedras.

Description: Quite a difficult walk with a steep descent of 700m

(2,300ft). For surefooted walkers only. **Time**: 2 hours.

How to get there and back: Bus 103 from Funchal to Boaventura as far as Santana at 7am. Journey time 2 hours 15 minutes. Go by taxi from Santana to the Achada do Teixeira. Arrange for the taxi to collect you from Pico das Pedras and take you to Santana for the 103 bus to Funchal at 1.30pm, 5.30pm.

Directions: At the far end of the car park by the Achada do Teixeira stands a rest house. Nearby is a viewpoint with some fine views over the north coast of the island. Look out for the Homem em Pé (Upright Man), a huge basaltic rock formation beneath the viewpoint. A flight of steps leads down past the rock to the grass below. This field path ends at the tarred road to Santana (25 minutes) and a few steep steps lead down to the road.

About 50m down this road on the left stands another viewpoint with railings and a made-up path branches off here.

This steep path, which can be very slippery in wet weather, runs steeply downhill through thick, lichen-covered heather bushes. The weather is often cloudy here, especially in winter, but the tree heath show its true face in these conditions and the path has its own special charm. In the quiet of summer listen out for the birds singing from the bushes.

After an arduous climb up a stony path you will reach a gateway (1 hour 15 minutes), but beyond here an easy, gently sloping path leads down to the thatched houses of Queimadas (1 hour 25 minutes). It is certainly worth taking a stroll through the extensive parkland, especially when the rhododendrons are in bloom during March. This state-owned holiday complex is not attended, but there is a large picnic site and a toilet block just below the houses.

The main path passes to the right of the houses as far as a junction (1 hour 30 minutes). Turn left here to the picnic site mentioned above or straight on along the made-up track to Santana, a 1½ hour walk away including a steep drop of about 500m (1,650ft). You may prefer an easier route via the forest lodge on Pico das Pedras, in which case turn right at the junction and join the mossy Levada do Caldeirão Verde with its wide track running alongside. You will soon pass a secluded picnic site (1 hour 35 minutes).

The path continues eastwards and without any perceptible gradient. It is almost impossible to lose your way here, but you should watch out for occasional large holes in the path. You will soon reach the road at the foot of Pico das Pedras (2 hours). Follow this road uphill for about 100m to the forest lodge, where another picnic site is situated.

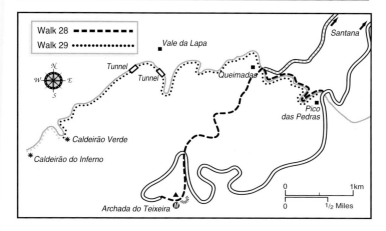

29 THE GREEN CAULDRON AND A WATERFALL

Pico das Pedras (forest lodge) - Queimadas - Caldeirão Verde

Save this quite complicated walk for a fine day. It leads to one of the most impressive spots on the island, the Green Cauldron (Caldeirão Verde). Start out from Pico das Pedras and follow the easy Levada do Caldeirão Verde as far as the thatched houses. After, the path narrows and on the right-hand side the rock face falls steeply into thickly wooded gorges. Lush laurel woodland lines the *levada*. Lichen, ferns and moss bear witness to the permanently high humidity in this cloudy region. The highlight of the walk is without doubt the Caldeirão Verde, an almost circular crater into which water tumbles from a height of about 100m (325ft). The sides of the crater, almost always wet and in shadow, are overgrown with green ferns.

Description: A difficult *levada* walk but without any appreciable gradients. Only for sure-footed walkers with a good head for heights. A torch for the tunnels is absolutely essential.

Time: 5 hours including the return journey.

How to get there and back: Take the 103 bus from Funchal to Boaventura as far as Santana, at 7am. Journey time 2 hours 15 minutes. Go by taxi to Pico das Pedras. Arrange to be collected by taxi from Pico das Pedras and taken to Santana. The 103 bus leaves Santana at 5.30pm.

Directions: About 100m below the forest lodge at Pico das Pedras, a signposted *levada* path turns off to the west to Queimadas. Taxi drivers know this spot. Carry straight on along a wide path between the oak trees. Look out for holes in the path. After a small, beautifully situated picnic site (25 minutes), you will reach a junction. Carry straight on for Queimadas park (see Walk 28).

Behind the picnic site, a bridge leads over a pond and a sign-post marks the way to the Caldeirão Verde. You will soon come to a *levada* path which you should follow. Carry straight on at the next junction (40 minutes), but the path narrows and there is a risk of slipping on the mossy *levada* wall. Water drips constantly on to the path from the overhanging rock. There is a path, very steep in places, down to the right and also a fence but this is broken in a number of places.

A beaten path (55 minutes) leads down to the right across a stream and then back up to the *levada* wall. This path avoids a particularly difficult section of the *levada*, which passes under a waterfall. Another stream higher up is crossed by a 6m (20ft) *levada* bridge (1 hour 15 minutes). The poorly secured path runs along a narrow ledge next to the *levada* wall and you may wish to hold on to this.

Pass a small wooden gate (1 hour 20 minutes) and then, shortly after, a waterfall comes into view under which the *levada* passes. However, before the path reaches the waterfall, it crosses over to the other side of the valley via a bridge. You will now come to the first tunnel (1 hour 40 minutes). It is not too long and if you keep your head well down, you can pass through it. Soon a path forks off to the right to the Vale de Lapa forest lodge, but you should turn left through a cut in the rock. Just beyond here is the start of the third tunnel, and this can also be traversed without too much difficulty.

A larger valley soon emerges allowing the Ribeira Grande to flow north into the Atlantic near São Jorge. Steep rock faces line the valley and in some places, where the *levada* wall is narrow and slippery, there is a risk of vertigo. You will pass through another short tunnel (2 hours 15 minutes). A side valley broadens out into a semi-circle and a wide almost dry river bed winds in from the left. Here a signpost indicates the route away from the *levada* to the Caldeirão Verde. Sometimes the sign is removed so it is important to look out for the stream. After just a few metres on a bumpy path, the Green Cauldron comes into view. It is an inviting place for a relaxing picnic, before the return journey. The *levada* continues on to the Caldeirão do Inferno, an awe-inspiring chasm about 30 minutes walk away. However, parts of the walk are in bad condition and unprotected.

Back in Queimadas, you can make a steep descent to Santana along a made-up road. The journey takes about 1½ hour. Turn right on the main road and it is not far to the town centre. This route makes a good alternative if you have not arranged to be collected by a taxi at the starting point near Pico das Pedras. In Santana you can wait for your bus in the 'O Colmo' restaurant.

30 A SCENE OF UNSPOILT RURAL TRANQUILLITY

Pico das Pedras (forest lodge) - Cabeço da Cova da Roda - Lombo Galego -
Ribeira Seca - Cruzinhas

The path leads from the forest lodge by Pico das Pedras to the village of Cruzinhas, on the road from Faial to Ribeiro Frio, but it is little used. This is a pity as there are not only some magnificent views over the north coast but in one of the remotest regions of the island lies an idyllic rural landscape, still largely untouched by the twentieth century. Also, the path is unaffected by the weather — an advantage if mist shrouds the higher northern slopes of the mountains.

Description: A walk of medium difficulty with a long gentle descent (650m/2,000ft) but an arduous ascent (150m/500ft). **Time**: 3 hours.
How to get there and back: Take the 103 bus from Funchal to Boaventura as far as Santana at 7am. Journey time 2 hours 15 minutes. Alternatively, take the 53 bus from Funchal to Faial via Machico at 10am (Monday-Saturday) or the 78 bus at 8am (Sunday). Journey time 2 hours. Go by taxi from Santana or Faial to the forest lodge at Pica das Pedras. Return to Funchal on the 103 bus from Cruzinhas at 2.15pm, 6.25pm. Journey time 1 hour 30 minutes. Alternatively, take the 103 bus to Faial from Cruzinhas at 3.15pm and then from Faial to Machico on the 53 bus at 3.30pm (Monday-Saturday) or the 78 bus at 5.30pm (Sunday).

Penha de Águia (Eagle Rock) from Cova da Rova

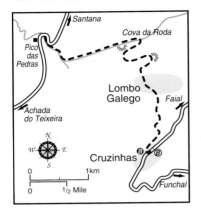

Directions: About 100m (110 yd) below the forest lodge at Pico das Pedras, the Levada do Caldeirão Verde crosses the road. If coming from Santana, take the *levada* path to the left, signposted to Faial. The *levada* is lined by hydrangea and runs through thin woodland, broken up by grassy meadows. An often overgrown path along a narrow *levada* forks off to the left (10 minutes). To carry straight on at this junction is not an option as the path is more or less impassable.

The narrow *levada* leads steeply downhill to a wide, easy path (25 minutes) at which you should turn left. A few lonely farmhouses will be found here and on the right between the bushes views from a panorama (30 minutes) extend from Faial to the island's eastern tip at Ponta da São Lourenço. At this level you are often just below the clouds which invariably cover Madeira's northern slopes. The path from here to Cruzinhas is not affected by weather conditions.

Follow the wide path as far as the junction at Cova da Roda, marked by a huge, impressive tree (40 minutes). Turn right to Cruzinhas along a grassy path down to a small low-lying meadow. Bear left at the fork (45 minutes) and shortly after cross the valley to another superb viewpoint (1 hour) to the imposing Eagle Rock.

The made-up path now runs through terraced fields, past thatched cow byres and on to the first houses at the edge of Lombo Galego. A tarred road (1 hour 20 minutes) forks to the left after a few houses, but keep straight on along the old path, which descends gently between the vegetable plots and scattered houses — some of which give a rather surprising impression of prosperity.

The lowest point in the walk is the river bed of the dry Ribeira Seca (2 hours 20 minutes). This valley is an important centre for the cultivation of willow cane for the basket-making industry and in spring the farmers can be seen harvesting and preparing their crop. The arduous haul up to Cruzinhas starts here. Although the road from Faial can be seen below, the first houses of Cruzinhas are still quite a long way off. Just up to the right is a simple café. A few metres to the left is the road from Faial to Ribeiro Frio (3 hours) where you will find the bus stop.

31 THE WILD COAST

Santana - Calhau de São Jorge - Ponta de São Jorge - Vigia - São Jorge

A little-used path runs along the north coast from Santana to São Jorge and until earlier this century, it was the main link between the two little towns and was used to carry goods from the jetty at São Jorge up to the regional centre of Santana. The path has fallen into disrepair and coastal erosion has also taken its toll in places. It is, nevertheless, an unusual walk for Madeira as it is one of the few places where it is possible to walk by the sea. The sparse vegetation of the rocky coastline remains unchanged. Starting out from Santana, the walk descends steeply into the Ribeira de São Jorge valley and then through the deserted settlement of Calhau, once the centre of the São Jorge parish and until World War II an important trading post. Keep going along the cliff tops to the tiny and now little-used harbour of São Jorge. Despite the strenuous climb up to the town, it is worth making the detour to the panorama at Vigia before coming to the centre of São Jorge with its baroque church.

Description: A walk of medium difficulty with climbs and descents of about 300m (1,000ft), parts of which can be quite slippery. Only for sure-footed walkers with a good head for heights. **Time**: 3 hours.

How to get there and back: Take bus 103 from Funchal to Boaventura as far as Santana (alight at the Venda Senhor Isidro bus stop) at 7am. Journey time 2 hours 15 minutes. Return on the 103 from São Jorge to Funchal at 1pm (Monday-Saturday), 5pm. Journey time 2 hours 45 minutes.

Directions: The bus stop is at the far end of Santana outside the shop (*venda*) of Senhor Isidro. This spot can easily be recognised by the statue of a black madonna, which stands before it on the left-hand side of the road. A wide track turns off to the right here, passes around a valley and then leads up to a cluster of trees. Just before the trees the path forks (20

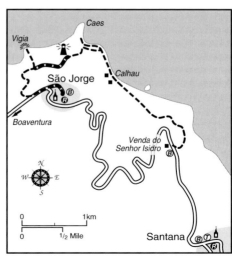

minutes) and then on the left the old, paved road to São Jorge begins its steep descent. In the background the São Jorge lighthouse can be made out high up on a rocky headland.

The path, badly overgrown in places, leads steeply down into the deep gorge of Ribeira de São Jorge and you will soon reach the foot of the valley (30 minutes). Here a long stone bridge, heavily overgrown with houseleeks, crosses the stream bed. Just beyond, the path forks. Bear left for the direct route up to São Jorge, but the coastal path to the right is much prettier. This way you will pass the few houses of the almost completely deserted village of Calhau and also small fields protected from the predominantly strong northerly winds by heather bushes. High waves crash against a lonely, offshore island.

At Calhau's last house the path forks again (1 hour). Keep to the right beside the sea. Here the path has been cut into the rock face and the surf has already to started to eat away at the path. Huge houseleeks grow on the rocks and down below the waves break on the stony beach. After passing a small bridge (1 hour 5 minutes) you will find that the path is buried under rubble and in places you will have to climb over fallen rocks. It soon gets easier and by a stone wall a path forks to the left (1 hour 20 minutes).

Make a mental note of this junction before continuing straight on along the coastal path. Ahead lies the dilapidated harbour of São

The landscape near Madeira's northern coast

Jorge. The small fishing boats, stowed away in a shed, are now only allowed over a step into the water on rare occasions in the summer. The hair-raising wooden bridge which leads to the harbour is sometimes broken by winter storms. At this point turn round and return to the last fork (1 hour 30 minutes). Take the steep right-hand path uphill. This path was once paved and carefully wound its way up the steep rock, supported by walls. But it, too, is now either buried under stones or has collapsed so that great care is needed.

Pass through a gate (1 hour 40 minutes) and keep straight on beside some vineyards. The path becomes a little easier and then bends round towards the first houses of São Jorge. The climb remains steep until you reach a wide field track (2 hours) which brings you up to the first cow byres and houses on the right. The path forks at a pink-washed house. Bear left towards a larger, white house. Keep left on the tarred road (2 hours 10 minutes) and bear left at the next fork. You will soon come to a small shop, which is also the village pub. The tarred road ends at the next junction (2 hours 25 minutes) and on the right a signpost shows the way to the Vigia viewpoint. The detour will take about 15 minutes but is well worth the effort as, on a clear day, it is possible to see right along the north coast as far as Porto Moniz. Until the 1980s this headland was used by the whalers of Caniçal as a look-out. When whales were sighted, a phone call alerted the boat crews in Caniçal.

Return to the last junction (2 hours 40 minutes) and keep straight on along a mud track, which keeps roughly at the same altitude, as far as the coast road (2 hours 55 minutes). Turn to the left for about 300m and walk as far as a junction where a road leads into the town centre. On the left, hidden away behind walls and tall trees, stands a delightful country house built by the famous Madeiran doctor and adventurer João Francisco de Oliveira. You will soon come to the main street of São Jorge. Turn right down to the church, where the bus stop and also a small bar are situated. The parish church should not be missed. It is a fine example of baroque style with some richly gilded carvings.

32 THROUGH CHERRY ORCHARDS TO THE CAPE

Estreito de Câmara - Ribeira da Caixa - Garachico - Cabo Girão - Cruz de Caldeirão

The area north of the Encumeada pass supplies the water for the Levada do Norte, whose water then feeds a number of smaller channels irrigating the coastal region between Ribeira Brava and Câmara de Lobos. The lower sections of the path which accompanies this narrow *levada* follow a sometimes dizzying course through

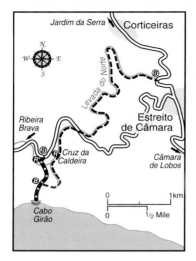

cherry orchards and terraced fields and without any obvious inclines. The extent to which the land is exploited can be appreciated as you look down towards the southern coast. The rows and rows of terraces enable farmers to make maximum use of the hillsides and are reminiscent of east Asia. The final destination for this walk is Cabo Girão, said to be the second highest sea cliff in the world, which towers some 578m (1,900ft) above the sea.

Description: A *levada* walk of medium difficulty without any appreciable gradients. A good head for heights is essential.

Time: 3 hours.

How to get there and back: Take the 96 bus from Funchal to Corticeiras as far as Estreito de Câmara de Lobos (Levada do Norte bus stop), every hour. Journey time 45 minutes. Return to Funchal on one of the buses which run along the southern coast road.

Directions: Situated by a vineyard on the left-hand side of the road opposite the bus stop, a small fight of steps leads down to the *levada*. Within the town the channel is covered with slabs, but it soon loses its cover and the walker has to make do with the narrow beaten path alongside. Pass by the tiny farmhouses, which have no link with the outside world other than this path, and also the countless terraced fields, each of which yields several different types of fruit.

Continue along the *levada* and past a fork, where a wide path branches off to the left (10 minutes). The narrow *levada* leads round a small valley in a wide arc. Leave the last houses of Estreito de Câmara behind you and enter a second, wider valley. Just beyond the bend, overhanging rocks block the path (25 minutes), but a beaten path leads down from the *levada* and bypasses this obstacle. Well-equipped and sure-footed walkers can follow the *levada* here, but will have to bend well down. After about 100m the beaten path rejoins the *levada*, which runs through cherry orchards into the Ribeira da Caixa valley. A wide but unprotected bridge crosses the stream (40 minutes). On the opposite slope, the path emerges from the valley through a sparse acacia wood.

The first houses of Garachico — a poor village where begging children are not uncommon — are visible beyond the next bend (1 hour). The women can often be seen working outside their front doors on Madeira embroidery and it is worth stopping to watch how the skilled hands replicate the complicated patterns.

The old *levada* path is interrupted by a road and you must climb some steps and cross the road to rejoin the *levada*. The *levada* now runs to the left behind a wash-house, on through sparse pine woodland and then soon after to a few houses (1 hour 30 minutes). The grounds of the waterhouse are usually barred by an iron gate and you will have to climb down to the left of the *levada*. A wide, made-up track a few metres away will return you to the *levada*. The water channel passes through pine forest and meets the main road from Funchal to Ribeira Brava (1 hour 40 minutes).

On the opposite side of the road stands a typically Madeiran red-tiled house with clay doves on the eaves — intended to ward off evil spirits. A few steps lead down to the *levada* here but you will need to take care shortly after, as the bridge which crosses the stream is often wet, slippery and without railings. Beyond, the *levada* runs high up on the hillsides and on the left side, a steep slope drops down into the valley below. There is a risk of vertigo here, despite the low-growing shrubs alongside the path.

The Levada do Norte emerges out of a tunnel (2 hours) on the western side of the mountain ridge. However, if you wish to finish your walk at the Cabo Girão do not pass through the tunnel but keep straight on at the *levada* junction. Further on beyond a few farm-houses, a track (2 hours 25 minutes) leads up to the car park at Cabo Girão (2 hours 35 minutes). Only a few metres away to the left a viewing platform stands at the edge of a sheer drop of 578m (1,900ft). Refreshments are available from a small bar on the car park, but only a short distance away lies Cruz da Caldeira (3 hours) with several bars, a supermarket and bus stop on the main street.

33 HIGH ABOVE THE SOUTH COAST
Boa Morte - Levada do Norte - Quinta Grande - Cruz da Caldeira
The section of the Levada do Norte west of Cabo Girão is less well known than the eastern section. This walk passes mainly through fragrant pine and eucalyptus woods, brightened in autumn by the pink flowers of the belladonna lilies. The soft soil of the woodland floor makes pleasant walking country and there are many fine views to be enjoyed over the fertile fields with their fruit, vegetables and sugar cane as well as over the rocky coastline.

Cabo Girão — one of the highest sea cliffs in the world

Description: A *levada* walk of medium difficulty without any appreciable gradients. Possibility of vertigo. **Time**: 3 hours.

How to get there and back: Take the 148 bus from Funchal to Boa Morte at 1pm (Monday-Friday). Journey time 1 hour 25 minutes. Alternatively, take the 7 bus to Ribeira Brava at 9.30am (Monday-Friday). Journey time 1 hour 30 minutes. From Ribeira to Boa Morte, take the 127 bus at 11.10am. Journey time 25 minutes. Return to Funchal on one of the buses which ply the southern coast road.

Directions: Take the road uphill from the bus terminus at Boa Morte. As you leave the village, the road enters a pine wood. Beyond a left-hand bend, you will pass a water-tank on the left-hand side and an isolated snack bar on the right (5 minutes) — so stop off now for refreshments or else buy your picnic to eat later on. About 100m behind the house, a wide track through the wood will bring you to the Levada do Norte (10 minutes). Turn right along the *levada* path, lined here with attractive flowers. The path runs alongside the *levada* without any appreciable gradients and often by the edge of the wood — pines and eucalyptus trees on the left, terraced fields with the occasional house on the right and the sea down below. Cross a road and a track in quick succession (45 minutes). Orange groves line the *levada*, before the watercourse passes into a wooded valley, where you will cross another track (1 hour). The church tower at Campanário suddenly comes into view (1 hour 25 minutes). A steep path crosses the *levada* and then you will have to use stepping stones to negotiate several streams.

The path now runs along the steep hillside, but it is quite safe. Two tracks cross the *levada* as it enters a small valley (2 hours 5 minutes) and at this point, the *levada* path is quite wide and concreted. Ahead lies the transmitter mast at the top of Cabo Girão and down below the coast road is visible, as the *levada* again runs along a steep slope. There is a short stretch of about 20m where a possibility of vertigo exists, but shrubs do grow on the right-hand side.

You will soon cross a paved path (2 hours 15 minutes) and here you can leave the *levada* and join the road near Quinta Grande, where there is a bus stop. The *levada* flows on

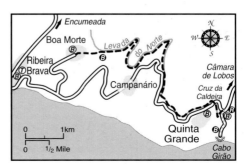

through a cut, beyond which it is bridged by a stream. A few metres before this, cross the *levada* and take a beaten path to the left up to the bridge (2 hours 25 minutes). Keep on following the *levada* path, pass a few houses and then walk along a 15m long, narrow wall. On the right, a ravine several metres deep can invoke feelings of vertigo.

A little further on lies the coast road and you should follow this uphill for about 50m across the bridge. Directly beyond the bridge, a beaten path leads down to the right through a narrow opening in a wall back to the *levada*. Turn left here and head towards Cabo Girão. Soon the *levada* disappears into a tunnel (2 hours 45 minutes) to the left but you should carry straight on along a narrow path to a steep pathway. This continues uphill to the coast road at Cruz da Caldeira (3 hours). A narrow road turns off here to Cabo Girão and you should allow about 25 minutes to the cape (see Walk 32).

34   THE LEVADA IN THE TABUA VALLEY

Ribeira Brava - Apresentação - Sitio da Ribeira - Candelária - Tábua - Ribeira Brava

This beautiful *levada* walk passes above Ribeira Brava through the Tabua valley to Candelária. After a steep ascent on an old, made-up road you will soon reach the Levada Nova which follows a straight-forward path apart from a few short, vertiginous stretches through the lush Tábua valley. From Candelária, descend to Tábua and from there along the coast back to Ribeira Brava.

Description: A *levada* walk of medium difficulty with ascents and descents of about 400m (1,300ft). Only for sure-footed walkers with a good head for heights. **Time**: 4½ hours.

How to get there and back: Take the 4 bus from Funchal to Ponta do Sol as far as Ribeira Brava at 10.05am (Monday-Saturday). Alternatively, take the 7 bus to Ribeira Brava at 9.30am (Monday-Friday), 10.05am (Sunday), 10.50am (Monday-Saturday). Journey time 1 hour 30 minutes. Return to Funchal from Ribeira Brava on the 6 bus at 4.30pm or the 7 bus at 3.30pm, 5.05pm, 6.35pm.

Directions: At the bus stop in Ribeira Brava, take the main road westwards. Before the river, the road to Encumeada turns off to the right. After about 100m turn left and cross the river. A few metres beyond the bridge, a flight of steps leads steeply up to the right, cutting off a bend in the road. When you rejoin the road (10 minutes), continue uphill high above the valley. After a left-hand bend another flight of steps leads steeply up a rock face (20 minutes) to a wide made-up path. Follow this down to the left for a short distance as far as a track (30 minutes).

The track runs to the right into the Caldeira valley. Once you have crossed this valley with its fields of sugar cane and bananas, a low wall will be visible on the left-hand side of the road. By the wall and the adjacent tiny pond, a made-up path leads up to the right between the gardens and banana plantations. Follow this path for quite a distance — it cuts off a number of bends, crossing the road four times. You should then look out for a brightly painted house with green and blue shutters on the right-hand side of the road. Just before the house, the Levada Nova (1 hour 10 minutes) branches off.

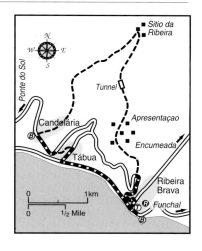

It approaches from below and can easily be missed.

The *levada* path passes leisurely between vineyards, vegetable plots and orange groves, affording many fine views over the coastal landscape. Beyond a curve, there is a risk of vertigo (1 hour 15 minutes) — the *levada* wall is only about 50cm (20in) wide and on the left, the drop is almost vertical. If necessary, you will have to walk through the water, but this dangerous section does not last long and soon the *levada* enters a small valley. Now and then you will see one of the traditional thatched houses, flowers line the path and in early spring the white trumpets of the arum lily are a delight.

A wide track crosses the *levada* (1 hour 30 minutes) and soon after you will reach a 50m long tunnel. No torch is required, but after the tunnel the *levada* runs along a steep rock face, although it is not particularly vertiginous. Beyond a cutting (1 hour 45 minutes) lies the far end of the Tábua valley. Cross a tarred road (2 hours) and, on the other side, steps lead down to the *levada*. Then you will reach a stream which in winter and after heavy rainfall cannot easily be crossed. A beaten path leads to the right up to a bridge and then returns to the *levada*.

Shortly after, you will need to wade across another stream and in winter this can be quite tiring. The *levada*, now much easier, leads out of the valley, although another stream has to be crossed (2 hours 10 minutes). The *levada* passes through dense woodland. In spring the acacia are in blossom and in summer clusters of blue-flowered agapanthus line the path. There are frequent views down into the

Banana plantations high above the southern coast

Levada Calheta is an easy walk in Madeira's unspoilt south-west

valley and out to sea. The valley becomes wider with more terraced fields as the first houses of

Candelária come into view (3 hours). The *levada* disappears by a made-up path, which descends steeply downhill. Follow this through the village as far as a bend in the road (3 hours 10 minutes). Continue to the left at first and then on a wide road round a right-hand bend. On the right-hand side, about 100m beyond the curve, a small white chapel, Senhora dos bons caminhos (Our Lady of the Good Paths) is set into the rock.

On the right lies Ponta do Sol with its old quay. You will soon reach the main road (3 hours 30 minutes) which runs to the left through the centre of the village. Beyond the village, a made-up path (3 hours 45 minutes) forks to the right down to Tábua. From Tábua, follow the main road down to the sea (4 hours 5 minutes) and then carry on along the new coast road to the left into Ribeira Brava (4 hours 30 minutes). If time allows, enjoy a drink at one of the cafés on the promenade while you wait for the bus.

35 MOUNTAIN RIDGE COUNTRY
Central Hidroeléctrica de Calheta - Ribeira do Raposa - Prazeres

The countryside at the western end of Madeira's south coast is rarely visited. In 1953 a *levada* was built from the electricity power station near Calheta westwards as far as Ponta do Pargo. For 500 years farmers here had to live with the risk of drought but now plentiful supplies of the precious liquid can be relied on. Countless streams have worn furrows in the coastal landscape, while narrow but steep mountain ridges known as *lombos* or *lombinhos* rise up in between. The *levada* meanders through the valleys with hardly any incline as far as the charming and unspoilt village of Prazeres.

Description: An easy *levada* walk without any appreciable gradients.
Time: 4 hours.
How to get there and back: Take bus 6 from Funchal to Boaventura as far as Ribeira Brava at 7.35am. Journey time 1 hour 20 minutes. Take a taxi to the 'Central Hidroeléctrica' near Calheta. Return to Funchal from Prazeres on the 107 bus at 3pm (Tuesday-Saturday). Journey time 3 hours 15 minutes. Alternatively take a taxi from Prazeres to Ribeira Brava and then take the 6 bus at 4.30pm or the 7 bus at 5.07pm, 6.35pm to Funchal. Journey time 1 hour 30 minutes.
Directions: The hydro-electric power station (Central Hidroeléctrica) at Calheta lies about 2km (1¼ miles) above the coast road. Find the *levada* behind the power station and follow it to the left in a westerly direction. After a short distance a made-up path leading up to the Paúl da Serra plateau crosses the *levada* (15 minutes). The path

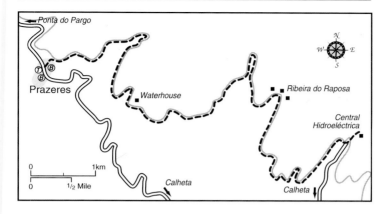

runs along the Lombo do Brasil ridge with rows of houses on either side, while the wet, shady valley floor is uninhabited. Carry on beside the *levada* which is soon crossed by another paved path (25 minutes). It too leads up to the Paúl da Serra along a ridge.

Follow the *levada* path through acacia, eucalyptus and pine woods with clusters of chestnut trees in between. In some of these remote valleys you will find remains of the original laurel woods. Pass beside the few houses in the hamlet of Ribeira do Raposa (50 minutes) and then the *levada* re-enters woodland. The path beside the *levada* is in good condition and there is no risk of vertigo.

Carry on past the little waterhouse at Atalhinho (2 hours 55 minutes) where an arm of the *levada* branches off to the left to Estreito da Calheta. A beautiful garden with flowers including roses, dahlias, agapanthus surrounds the house. Carry on along the main *levada* which meanders around more valleys and ridges until a small plateau comes into view (3 hours 45 minutes). Here, surrounded by terraced fields, the houses in Prazeres nestle around the church of Nossa Senhora das Neves. Above Prazeres, a track crosses the *levada* (3 hours 55 minutes). Follow this down to the main street. The bus stop can be found in the centre of the village, a few metres along on the left of the main street (4 hours).

36   THE SUNNY LEVADA
Reservoir (turning to Rabaçal) - Levada do Paúl - Cristo Rei

If the weather is fine, the best way to get to know the Paúl da Serra is by taking a walk along the Levada do Paúl. Starting from a high point at the eastern end, this carries water from the edge of the

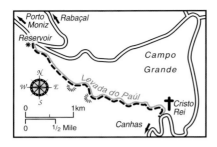

plateau as far as the reservoir at Rabaçal. The water is then fed through to the hydro-electric power station at Calheta before irrigating the fields along the southern coast. The *levada* path is simple and easy to walk. The barren landscape would be dull were it not for the fine views over the sea which lies over a thousand metres below.

Description: An easy *levada* walk without any appreciable gradients.

Time: 1 hour.

How to get there and back: Take the 107 bus from Funchal to Raposeira as far as Canhas (Recta das Canhas) at 8.05am. Journey time is 2 hours. From Canhas take a taxi to the Levada do Paúl reservoir near the turning to Rabaçal. Arrange with the taxi driver to be collected at Cristo Rei (Levada do Paúl) and then driven to Canhas. Return to Funchal on the 107 bus at 4.15pm (Tuesday-Saturday). Alternatively, take the taxi to Ribeira Brava and the 6 bus at 4.30pm or the 7 bus at 3.30pm, 5.05pm, 6.35pm.

Directions: On the left-hand side of the road to Porto Moniz which crosses the Paúl da Serra plateau lies a water tank or reservoir. It can be found near a narrow turning to the right towards Rabaçal. Opposite the junction and quite close to the road you will see the Levada do Paúl, which flows into the water tank. A pipe then feeds the water to Calheta. Follow the level, mainly grassy path which runs alongside the *levada* to the left or eastwards. The *levada* continues high up on the hillsides above the south-west coast just below the Paúl da Serra plateau. On a clear day the coastline below is visible but, during the course of the day, clouds often form about half-way up the slopes, blocking or impeding the downward view, while the hill tops remain bathed in glorious sunlight.

The terrain slopes gently down to the coast and vegetation on both sides of the *levada* is sparse, although occasionally cows can be seen grazing on the poor grass. A few shrubs hide in the narrow gullies or rock niches. Larger caves are used as shelters by the shepherds.

The *levada* now gently, almost imperceptibly, winds its way up around the hillside and then suddenly a statue of Christ, Cristo Rei,, comes into view above the path. Shortly after you will join the road (1 hour) from Canhas to the Paúl da Serra plateau, where the taxi should be waiting.

37   PANORAMIC VIEWS FROM THE PLATEAU

Campo Grande - Chapana - Ribeira Seca - Bica da Cana

Bica da Cana means 'a small spring where reeds grow' but there are in fact many springs to be found in the region surrounding the mountain. Set out from Campo Grande and cross the barren Paúl da Serra plateau following on an old, road builders' track to the round summit at the eastern end of the plateau. Bica de Cana at 1,620m (5,313ft) is one of the highest points on the Paúl da Serra. In the east the terrain falls steeply down to the Encumeada pass, affording an unimpeded view over the central highland peaks. To make the most of this walk, wait for a sunny day.

Description: An easy *levada* walk with a gentle climb of about 200m (650ft) on a wide, stony path. **Time**: 1½ hour.

How to get there and back: See Walk 36 for details of how to get from Funchal to Canhas. Take a taxi from Canhas to the Paúl da Serra road sign on the Campo Grande. Arrange to be collected by taxi from Bica da Cana. To return to Funchal from Canhas or Ribeira Brava by bus, see Walk 36.

Directions: Situated on the road from Canhas to Porto Moniz and just beyond a tall statue of Christ a sign marks the start of the Paúl da Serra. A wide track branches off to the right at that point and a narrow field path soon crosses the track (5 minutes), followed by a fork (10 minutes). Both paths meet up again after about 100m (110yd), although the right-hand path is more direct. Just beyond lies a small quarry and the path starts to climb a little. On both sides moss and ferns clothe the barren landscape, which is level apart from a flat peak ahead. At the next junction (15 minutes), bear left slightly along the wider track and head for the summit which should be directly in

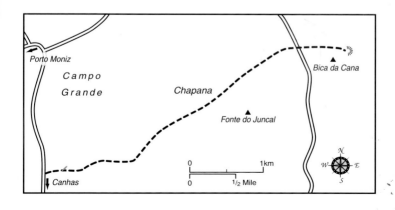

front. Another path joins from the right (25 minutes) and the route then follows the edge of the plateau. To the right you can peer deep into a valley and look out to the south coast beyond. The path is stony at this point and only just passable so keep to the edge of the track.

You will cross a narrow cutting and from then on keep to the flat gorge with a higher peak on the right and a lower round hilltop on the left and as you leave the steep ledge behind. At a fork (45 minutes) keep to the right along the wide path and continue into the valley. The path divides again and you should take the left fork along the dry river bed at the foot of the valley.

A few houses suddenly come into view (55 minutes) and trees cluster around this small settlement. Behind it rises the rocky round summit of Bica da Cana. To get there you must cross another valley floor. First make your way to the left along the wide path, cross the river bed (1 hour) and then you will find an opening in the fence, which divides up grazing land. Beyond here follow the road which is clearly visible now.

When you have reached the road (1 hour 10 minutes), the climb up to the Bica da Cana panorama starts. Keep straight on along a made-up track and, just before some houses, turn to the left on a wide path which then winds its way up to the viewing terrace (1 hour 30 minutes). This overlooks first the São Vicente valley, the solitary Rosário bell-tower and then the whole of the central highlands.

38   TO THE DOUBLE WATERFALL
Rabaçal - Risco waterfalls

The slopes to the north of the Paúl da Serra plateau drop steeply down to the thickly wooded valley of the Ribeira da Janela. Here, much of the island's original vegetation remains almost untouched. At a higher level where the Levada do Risco starts, thick clusters of tree-high heathers can be seen and their small white flowers brighten the landscape in early spring. The two Risco waterfalls tumble down from the plateau more than 100m (325ft) above, supplying the *levada* of the same name with water. In winter they make an impressive sight.

Description: A light *levada* walk without any appreciable gradients.
Time: 45 minutes including the return journey.
How to get there and back: See Walk 36 for details of how to get from Funchal to Canhas. Take a taxi from Canhas to Rabaçal. Arrange with the taxi driver to be collected at Rabaçal and driven to Canhas or Ribeira Brava and from there to Funchal by bus (see Walk 36).
Directions: The narrow road to Rabaçal ends at a car park above a

cluster of state-owned holiday homes. The path to the Risco waterfalls begins by the highest house, where a narrow path on the right leads steeply down to the Levada do Risco (5 minutes).

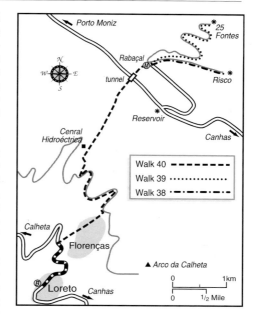

Follow the watercourse to the right along a wide, mossy path under huge spreading tree heaths. Look for fish in the clean *levada* which has been stocked for anglers.

The waterfalls at 25 Fontes are signposted down to the left, but carry straight on along the *levada* path (10 minutes). After a short distance, the tree heath wood clears and the two adjacent Risco waterfalls lie directly ahead. Ignore the path on the left, which leads steeply downhill, as it is possible to carry on along the damaged *levada* wall. Badly overgrown with moss, the wall is constantly splashed by the many springs which bubble from the rock wall. From here onwards, there is not only the risk of getting wet — the path is also quite slippery and dangerous.

It is better to enjoy to the full the view of the waterfalls and the Ribeira da Janela valley before returning to Rabaçal on the *levada* footpath. Take some time to have a closer look at the thatched huts. An overnight stay is only possible if a reservation has been made in the Quinta Vigia in Funchal and even so, the accommodation is unattended. Toilets can be found in the lowest block. To get there pass around the highest house in a clockwise direction and then follow the steps downhill.

39 TWENTY-FIVE SPRINGS

Rabaçal - 25 Fontes

Only in recent decades has the Ribeira da Janela valley been opened up by levadas. Many waterfalls cascade from the rainy northern side of the Paúl da Serra plateau and supply the Levada das 25 Fontes and the higher Levada do Risco with water. Both levadas link up at Rabaçal and run through a tunnel to the hydro-electric power station at Calheta above the south-western coast. These levadas were built over largely inaccessible terrain and some extremely steep slopes. Today, as walkers stroll along paths with only the slightest of inclines, few will appreciate the dangers the builders faced. A risk of vertigo does exist in some places along the Levada das 25 Fontes. The waterfalls at 25 Springs (Vinte e cinco fontes) are one of nature's showpieces.

Description: A *levada* walk of medium difficulty with a steep ascent and descent of about 80m (260ft). Only for sure-footed walkers with a good head for heights. **Time**: 2 hours including return journey.

How to get there and back: See Walk 38

Directions: Set out from the car park at Rabaçal. Follow the directions for Walk 38 as far as the signpost (10 minutes) and then turn left down towards 25 Fontes. A flight of steps in the rock leads down through thick tree heath wood and to the Levada das 25 Fontes (20 minutes). Turn right here but remember the spot for the return journey.

Carry on along the *levada* path which initially is quite wide. A flight of steps leads down to a bridge (35 minutes). Cross a narrow gorge, its waters rushing from the Risco waterfalls. Beyond the bridge, climb a few steps and pass a small waterhouse. The *levada* path then narrows and in some places on the left-hand, there is a steep drop. Do not walk on the *levada* wall, but below it to one side. A slight risk of vertigo exists here.

In many places, there is an uninterrupted view over the green and densely wooded Ribeira da Janela valley but, from this point on, it is completely inaccessible. Soon you will reach another small bridge (1 hour). Just before the bridge a narrow path leads off to the right into the undergrowth. After a few metres it opens out into a shady, semi-circular basin valley into which one large and several smaller waterfalls cascade, namely the 25 Springs. The water collects in a small lake and in summer it serves a swimming pool for local people.

On the return journey look out for the turning up to the left to the Levada do Risco (1 hour 40 minutes). If you miss it, you can continue as far as the *levada* tunnel entrance (1 hour 55 minutes) and then climb to the left up to the houses in Rabaçal.

40 THE VALLEY OF THE LEVADAS

Rabaçal - Florenças - Loreto

This magnificent walk ventures into hidden Madeira. It starts in Rabaçal by the holiday centre north of the main mountain ridge. Beyond the tunnel for the combined Levada do Risco and Levada das 25 Fontes, it follows the southern slopes of the Paúl da Serra through scrub and pine woods, above the Calheta power station and then alongside the *levada* that carries the water eastwards and down to the fields. Before dropping steeply down to Loreto, the path peacefully follows a flower-lined *levada*.

Description: A *levada* walk of medium difficulty with a descent of almost 700m (2,300ft). Only for the sure-footed. A torch is required for the tunnel. **Time**: 2½ hours.

How to get there and back: See Walk 38. Return to Funchal on the 107 bus from Loreto at 3.45pm. Journey time 2 hours 30 minutes.

Directions: Beneath the car park at Rabaçal lie the state-run holiday

Agapanthus grow alongside many of the levadas

homes. Pass the highest house on the left and then take a flight of steps on the right down to the Levada das 25 Fontes (10 minutes). Turn left, cross a bridge and continue as far as an expanse of grass. This is where the long tunnel through to the south coast begins. As long as you have a torch it is easy to negotiate. It ends in Calheta valley (20 minutes) and some workmen's sheds can be seen just past the tunnel exit.

Continue briefly to the left alongside the *levada* as far as a narrow bridge which spans a stream. Just beyond the bridge the path forks and you should head downhill away from the *levada*. The path now runs through low-growing shrubs and leaves the *levada* well behind. There are some fine views down into the valley. Cross a few water pipes and soon you will join the Levada da Rocha Vermelha (45 minutes). Follow it to the left as far as a water basin where it ends and then descend the adjoining narrow path.

At a junction (55 minutes) either carry straight on along the narrow path or turn right down a wide track. They meet up about 100m (110yd) further on. You will soon pass a number of terraced fields and cow sheds beside the made-up path which follows and then you will join the *levada* (1 hour 5 minutes) which carries the water from the Calheta power station eastwards. Follow this *levada* eastwards and enjoy the fine views down to the south coast and, in early spring, the sight of the acacias in bloom. Negotiate two small valleys and then at an abandoned house turn to the right along a made-up road (1 hour 40 minutes). This runs steeply downhill to the main road (2 hours 5 minutes). Turn left and carry on as far as the main square and church at Loreto (2 hours 30 minutes) where the bus stop is situated. The church is usually closed but the south portal is worth a quick look as it is a fine example of Manueline architectural style.

Madeira Fact File

Accommodation

Holiday travel operators can usually offer a range of accommodation in hotels and self-catering apartments of medium to high quality. Most accommodation is in Funchal, the best location for walking holidays, but other centres such as Caniço/ Garajau and Machico can offer excellent hotels. Independent travellers will be able to find less expensive hotels and *pensions* in these places too. The tourist office at the airport or a friendly taxi driver can usually help to find rooms as well. If you wish to book independently the Portuguese Tourist Board can supply a full list of accommodation.

Walkers may like to consider some other options outside the main tourist areas. There are hotels and *pensions* in Ribeira Brava, Porto Moniz, São Vicente, Santana, Santo da Serra and Santa Cruz. In addition, the two state-owned hotels (*pousadas*) at Vinháticos near Serra da Água, and on the summit of Pico do Arieiro make excellent starting points for walks. There is a restricted number of beds available at these hotels but accommodation can be booked in advance from the UK. Some package tours include a week with car hire and stays at Pico do Arieiro, Vinháticos and São Vicente, followed (or preceded) by a week in Funchal.

Beds in the mountain huts at Pico Ruivo have to be reserved at the Tourist Information Office in Funchal. No meals are provided and the same is true of the state-owned huts in Queimadas and Rabaçal. They are only open in the summer and reservation is only possible through the Regional Government Office at Quinta Vigia in Funchal.

Although most package tours are based in Funchal, the more enterprising operators offer a week-long 'Pousada Tour', which has accomodation at Pico do Arieiro, São Vicente and Vinháticos and includes car hire. Followed or preceded by a week in Funchal, this makes an ideal way of seeing the different aspects of the island.

The island's only campsite is situated in Porto Moniz and it is open all year round. Campers often erect tents near the state-owned holiday villages in Queimadas and Rabaçal and use the

toilets and showers. Unauthorised camping is generally tolerated, although not welcomed. Please respect the countryside!

Climate

Even during the 'rainy season' when up to 3,000mm (120in)
can fall in the north-west and only 550mm (21in) in the south,
heavy downpours only occur occasionally and it will not be
long before the sun re-emerges. On average, rain falls on forty-
eight days of the year, ten of which are in November and about
five each in the other winter months with the remaining rainy
days shared out fairly evenly, although July and August are
usually the driest months. Often misty clouds surround the
island and the higher regions and even at midday clouds
shroud the mountain peaks. In summer, the *leste*, a hot, dry
wind, blows over Madeira from the Sahara for one, three or
five days.

February is the coolest month with average temperatures of
15°C (59°F), while visitors in August and September can expect
temperatures of around 22°C (71°F). Temperatures rarely ex-
ceed 30°C (86°F).

Sea water temperatures hover around 18°C (64°F) with lows
in winter of 16°C (60°F) and highs in summer of 22°C (71°).

The Tourist Office in Funchal has daily weather reports.

Clothing & Walking Equipment

For Madeira pack the clothes you would need for a British
summer holiday and including a warm jumper and a water-
proof. Remember that the weather at sea-level in Madeira can
be very different to conditions on the mountain tops and that
warm clothes should always be taken on any excursions
inland. July and August are the only months when there is
virtually no rainfall, so an anorak or cagoule is advisable and
should be carried with you. Showers can occur with little
warning. In Funchal many of the pavements are cobbled and
uneven, so strong, well-soled shoes are advisable even for the
less adventurous.

Shoes for the shingly and rocky beaches are worth including, as are trainers with moulded soles. These will be useful on
short walks in the hills or around the town. Down by the coast
light summer chlothing should suffice. Inland be prepared for

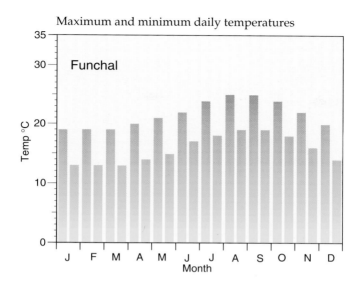

Maximum and minimum daily temperatures

Funchal

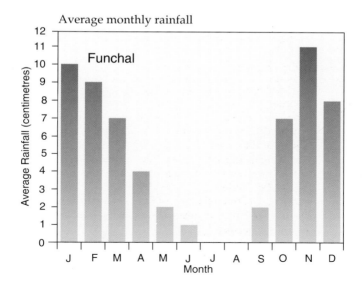

Average monthly rainfall

Funchal

changing weather conitions, especially if you are walking in the mountains. A stout pair of shoes is important, but walking shoes, better still mountain boots, are essential for the mountain paths. A thick pullover is essential in winter and an anorak is vital whatever the season — the type that can be folded away compactly in a rucksack is best. Also carry protection from rain and sun as the weather is unpredictable. It is always a good idea to include a drink, something to eat and a first aid kit when preparing for a walk. A torch may also be needed for certain walks which pass through tunnels. A small rucksack is a more convenient way of carrying essential belongings than a hand or shoulder bag.

Currency

The currency is the Portuguese escudo (abbreviated to Esc. or $) which is subdivided into 100 centavos, but the centavo is falling into disuse now as it is worth so little.

There are bank notes for 20, 50, 100, 500, 1,000 and 10,000 escudos and coins in denominations of 1, 2.50, 5, and 25 escudos. 1,000 escudos are known as 1 conto.

It is better to change money in the UK than to wait until you arrive in Madeira. In addition, a maximum of only 5,000 escudos may be imported or exported, but there are no similar restrictions on non-Portuguese currencies. Eurocheques are widely accepted.

Bank opening times: Monday-Friday 8.30-11.45am, 1-2.45pm; Saturday 8.30-11.45am. Bureaux de change are usually open all day and at weekends.

Consulate

British Consulate
14 Rua da Sé
Funchal
☎ 221221

Customs allowances

Tourists are not usually restricted, but only articles for personal use on holiday may be taken into Portugal duty-free. The same applies for the return journey to the UK.

Electricity

The volyage is 220v AC and uses continental two-pin plugs, so an adaptor is necessary for UK or US plugs.

Emergencies

In case of emergencies your hotel reception should be able to help you, otherwise telephone 115 for police (Polcia), ambulance (Ambulancia), or fire brigade (Bombereiros).

The tourist police may be called upon for assistance. They wear a uniform with green and red stripes on the arms, a badge with the word 'Turismo' and they can speak English. They are there to offer general advice and also to help with directions.

Food and Drink

Food can be bought from supermarkets in the tourist centres and bigger towns, but in villages, simple shops offer little other than bread, bananas, cheese and drinks.

Restaurants can be found in Funchal, Caniço and Machico but most Madeirans cannot afford to eat out and, away from the main centres, there are only the country 'inns' which cater for the local people and tourists. However, most of these will offer Madeiran specialities such as beef kebabs (*espetada*), swordfish (*espada*) or tuna (*atún*). Fish soup (*caldeirada da peixe*), another popular and tasty dish, contains various types of fish, potatoes, tomatoes and onions. Starters usually include tomato soup or fish soup, while fresh fruit, ice cream or one of the very sweet but delicious 'puddings' appear on most dessert menus. Where appropriate, restaurants are mentioned in the walks.

Bars, on the other hand, can be found in the remotest of places and usually offer meals — often very reasonably priced. Drinkers will usually stand at the bar and such places tend to be frequented by men, but the old traditions are slowly changing. The favourite drink of the locals is a cheap, light, red wine produced in large quantities on the north coast, but the local beer (Coral) is also good. Mineral water and the excellent locally-made *brisa* lemonade are ideal for anyone in search of a non-alcoholic drink. *Aguardente* is a popular brandy, distilled from grapes or sometimes even from sugar cane (*aguar dente de cana*). Madeiran liqueurs are very good too. Look out particularly for an aromatic passion fruit liqueur. Mention should also made here of the world-renowned madeira wine, a fortified wine similar to port or sherry and drunk either as an aperitif or a dessert wine.

Coffee is readily available and is the most popular choice for Madeirans at home or in a bar when meeting friends. *Bica*, a type of coffee similar to espresso, is usually drunk with a lot of sugar. Milky coffee is called *chinesa* — a term you will only encounter on Madeira. Tea is rarely drunk and, when it is offered, poorly prepared.

The water is safe to drink, but it has a high mineral content and strong taste. Bottled water, either still (*sem gas*) or sparkling (*com gas*) is readily available in supermarkets.

Health

If you are taking any medication, make sure you have adequate supplies for your stay. However, you can be confident of finding well-stocked chemists and medical centres on Madeira.

There are health centres in most towns and large villages, but hospitals are only to be found in Funchal. If you need to use the health services (Serviços de Saúde) visitors from EC countries should present form E111 to

Centro de Saúde do Bom Jesus
Serviço de Migrantes
Rua ds Hortas 67
9000 Funchal
☎ 29161 ext 2816/7
Office hours: Monday-Friday 9.30am-12noon, 2-4pm

Language

The language of Madeira is Portuguese, the same as the language of the mother country, 900km (560miles) away. Some knowledge of Spanish will certainly help, but in Funchal which is geared to tourism, English is usually understood and, in places, French as well. However, outside the main tourist areas — even though it is only a small island — difficulties with understanding can occur.

Pronunciation of the Portuguese language can be difficult

174

given the many nasal sounds. Listen carefully to how the word 'São', (Spanish San) is spoken and you will very quickly be able to say it as one syllable. With one or two exceptions, the pronunciation of the each letter is the same as English.

Stress is usually placed on the penultimate syllable when the word ends in a vowel and on the last syllable when ending with 'l' or 'r'. If the stress falls elsewhere, the syllable to be emphasised is shown with an accent.

The following expressions may be of use, especially to walkers.

Bom dia	Hello (before about 1pm)
Boa tarde	Hello (after about 1pm)
Por favor	Please.
Obrigado	Thank you (used by men).
Obrigada	Thank you (used by women).
Sim	Yes.
Não	No.
Onde é o caminho para ...?	Where is the path to ...?
Onde é a estrada para ...?	Where is the road to ...?
Onde é a paragem?	Where is the bus stop?
Preciso dum taxi para ...?	I need a taxi to ...
Procuro um bon restaurante	I'm looking for a good restaurant
Um Bilhete para ...	A ticket to ...
Quanto custa?	How much does it cost?
Quando parte a camioneta para ...?	When does the bus to ... leave?
Quando chega a camioneta em ...?	When does the bus arrive in ...?
A uma hora	At one o'clock
As duas, três, quatro	At two, three, four
cinco, seis, sete, oito	five, six, seven, eight
nove, dez, onze	nine, ten, eleven o'clock
Ao meio-dia	At 12 noon
As duas e meia	At half past two
As duas e um quarto	At quarter past two
A um quarto para as duas	At a quarter to two
segunda-feira	Monday
terça-feira	Tuesday
quarta-feira	Wednesday
quinta-feira	Thursday
sexta-feira	Friday

sábado	Saturday
domingo	Sunday
amanhã	tomorrow
á direita	right
á esquerda	left
á direito	straight on
em frente	straight on
Quantos quilómetros são até ...?	How many kilometres to ...?
por baixo	below
em cima	above
aquí	here
lá	there

Some Madeiran expressions:

Levada (irrigation channel): The whole island is criss-crossed with channels which carry water from the wet northern slopes to the southern side of the island in order to irrigate the banana plantations and vineyards. Well-maintained paths run alongside the levadas and are ideal for walking.

Quinta (country mansion): Walkers will frequently pass these country homes which belong mainly to wealthy islanders. Most were built during the last century in the English colonial style and are invariably surrounded by extensive parkland with a collection of various exotic plants.

Miradouro (viewing platform): These viewpoints in prominent locations are usually surrounded by carefully-tended flowerbeds. They are found not just by the roadside but also along many country paths.

Palheiro (thatched huts): Cow sheds built in the traditional style, originally with a thatched roof that extended on both sides almost down to the ground. As the thatch needed to be renewed every few years, the roofs are now often replaced with corrugated metal sheets. They can be seen almost everywhere between the terraced fields and usually house one or two cows.

Ribeiro (stream): These fast-flowing streams have cut deep gorges through the rock. While they undoubtedly add to the beauty of the island, until recently they made access to the interior very difficult. The streams on the south side of the island normally dry up in the summer, while on the north side water flows all the year round.

Maps & Books

Topographical maps of Madeira are usually out of date due to the number of new roads which are being built, or tracks being improved, with the help of EC grants. Finding your way with this book should not to prove too difficult, although a road map is recommended. A free map is obtainable from the Tourist information Office in Funchal, and this is quite adequate. Tourist maps produced by Clyde Leisure or Bartholemew (both with multi-lingual text) are recommended and are available in local shops. A pictorial relief map is available on the island, and although not recommended as a road map, it does give a very good impression of the topography of Madeira, Funchal and Porto Santo.

Books on Madeiran flora will undoubtedly be useful and they can usually be bought from souvenir shops or in the Tourist Information Office in Funchal. António da Costa and Luis de O. Franquinho's Madeira: *Plants and Flowers* is an excellent multilingual guide to the island's flora and it has many colour illustrations.

Opening Hours

Municipal buildings are open: 9am-12.30pm, 2-5pm.
Shops are open: Monday- Friday 9am-1pm, 3-7pm; Saturday 9am-1pm, but shops which rely heavily on tourism often have longer opening hours.
Chemists are open: 9am-1pm, 3-7pm.

Passports

A valid passport is required for entry into Madeira. For stays longer than two months, a visa is required. Apply to the Portuguese consulate.

Public Holidays

1 January	New Year
25 April	Day of the Revolution
1 May	Worker's Day
10 June	National holiday in honour of Luis Camões
15 August	Feast of the Assumption

5 October	Remembrance Day in honour of heroes of the Republic
1 November	All Saints' Day
1 December	Independence Day
8 December	Feast of the Immaculate Conception
25 December	Christmas Day

Movable feasts include Shrove Tuesday, Good Friday, Easter and Corpus Christi

Newspapers

As well as the local *Diário Notícias* in Portuguese, there is the *Madeira Island Bulletin*, a free monthly paper in English which has useful information for the visitor.

Postal Services & Telephones

The post office is responsible for the post, telephones and telegram service and you can make long-distance calls from booths where you pay after the call is finished. The main post office in the centre of Funchal is in Avenida da Zarco, with another in Rua da Ribeira de São João. The main post offices are open Monday-Friday 8.30am-8pm, Saturday 8.30-12.30pm. There is also a post office at the Lido complex, open: Monday-Friday 9am-7pm.

Post offices in smaller towns and villages are open shorter hours. They sell stamps and the cards used in public telephones. Stamps can also be bought from shops displaying a *Correios* sign. Post boxes also have the word *Correio*, while blue post boxes marked *Correio Azul* are for express mail and need extra postage.

There are no area telephone codes on Madeira. The code for the island is 351 91. From the UK prefix this with 010.

Shopping

The urge to shop can always be satisfied. Prices are fixed and although goods are not always cheap, tourists will not be 'ripped off'. Certainly worth a mention is the Casa do Turista with its tastefully decorated sales hall and the rustic courtyard where Madeiran handicrafts are displayed.

Cayres, the biggest store on the island, situated north of the old town in Rua Dr F. Ornelas has a selection of popular arts and crafts and is a popular tourist shopping centre. A smaller version is located in the Centro Comercial Infante, a shopping arcade in Avenida de Arriaga.

Hotel boutiques often have a wealth of souvenirs and gifts on offer but these shops, like similar outlets throughout the world, are invariably pricey.

Sports

On a warm, sunny island, watersports will be high on many holidaymakers' agenda with swimming, diving, sailing, water-skiing, boat trips, angling and deep-sea fishing all easily arranged. Then there is golf, mini-golf and tennis, even motor-rallying or hunting (for rabbits, pheasants, snipe, quail or pigeons) as well as walking. However, plenty of the former and a little of latter will meet the needs of most families. Bull-fighting is still popular, but in Portugal the bull is not killed, so you can enjoy the action without fearing the worst. The arena is situated in the west of Funchal. Sunday afternoon in the Barreiros stadium is the usual time for football. Roller hockey is played in the Parque de Jogos. The following can provide infotmation:

Mountaineering, Mountain Walking
Tourist Information Office
Avenida de Arriaga 18, Funchal

There are no professional mountain guides, however the Tourist Office can call on local people with a thorough knowledge of the area.

Tennis
Many hotels have their own tennis courts.

Golf Courses
Santo da Serra (18 holes)
Campo de Golf da Madeira
Sto António de Serra
9200 Machico
☎ 552345/552356/552321
28km (17miles) from Funchal. The bigger hotels are affiliated to the golf club so guests can play there free of charge.

Palheiro (18 holes)
Quinta do Palheiro Ferreiro

Sailing
Boats (mostly dinghies) can be hired from Yachtclub, Rent-a-Boat and Amigos do Mar at the Cais Regional.

Sea-fishing, diving
Amigos do Mar, Funchal
Dom Petro Hotel, Machico
Hotel Galomar, Caniço de Baixo

Waterskiing, windsurfing
Contact Rent-a-Boat or Amigos do Mar in Funchal.
The Dom Pedro Hotel in Machico has its own windsurfing school.

Swimming
Most new hotels in Funchal have their own swimming pools. Sometimes, guests at hotels without pools are allowed to use the pools in neighbouring establishments.
Club de Turismo, Estrada Monumental. Park with swimming pool, almost 2km (1¼ miles) west of the town.
Lido, swimming pool complex, Estrada Monumental, a good 2km (1/4 miles) west of the town.
Clube Naval, Estrada Monumental, Ajuda, about 3km (2miles) west of the town. Saltwater pool and sea-bathing with water-sports.

Time Zone

The time in Madeira corresponds to Greenwich Mean Time, which is one hour behind Central European Time.

Tipping

A service charge is usually included in the bill. If guests have received particularly good service, then a tip of 500 Esc. would be gratefully received by the room maid or the waiter/waitress. In restaurants, a tip of about 10 per cent is normal, while taxi drivers expect about 5 per cent.

Tourist Information Offices

Local Tourist Offices
Avenida de Arriaga 18
9000 Funchal
☎ 229057/8
Open: Monday-Saturday 9am-7pm

Avenida Henrique Vieira de Castro
9400 Porto Santo
☎ 982361

Portuguese National Tourist Offices:
UK
22-25a Sackville Street
London
W1X 1DE
☎ 0171 4941441

USA
590 Fifth Avenue
New York
NY 10036
☎ 212 354 4403

Canada
500 Sherbrooke West
Suite 930
Montreal Quebec
H3A 3C3
☎ 514 843 4623

4120 Yonge Corporate Centre
Suite 414
Willowdale
Toronto
Ontario
M2P 2BP
☎ 416 250 7575

Tours & Organised Walks

Most package tours organise coach tours of the island. Among the companies which provide full day, half day and evening minibus tours is:
Madeira Express
38-40A Avenida Arriaga
Funchal
☎ 225250/227780

Two-day (Thursday/Friday or Saturday/Sunday) guided walks in the mountains with an English-speaking mountain guide are available. Pick-up and return is from the tourist hotels in Funchal or Machico, with an overnight stay at the *pousada* on Pico do Arieiro. Contact:
Pousada do Pico do Arieiro
Apart° 478
.9006 Funchal,
☎ 48188/48198

Guided levada walks (with pick-up from the tourist hotels) are organised by:
Soc de Animação Turistica LDA
Sitio da Igreja
9135 Camacha
☎ 922288

Travel

Getting there
By far the easiest way to get to Madeira is to book a package tour with a travel agent, which will include a charter flight to Funchal. Independent travellers should contact Air Portugal (TAP) for information on scheduled flights from major airports. If you wish to include Lisbon on your itinerary, fly direct to Lisbon and then take a ferry on to Madeira. The journey takes two days. Some air tour operators include a sightseeing stopover in Lisbon as part of a package holiday.

The airport on Madeira is approximately 10km/6 miles east of Funchal:
Santa Catarina Airport
☎ 524972/524941

Transport on the Island

Buses

The most economical way of getting about on Madeira is certainly the bus, but the network does look rather confusing. There are several bus companies (the Funchal town buses are orange) and each one serves a different part of the island. The terminus for most services is the promenade in Funchal or Rua Profitas near the market, but some depart from near the main post office on Rua São João. A brochure produced by the Tourist Information Office with details, of all the services that visitors may need, will sort out most difficulties. Tickets are usually bought on the bus from the driver, but weekly tourist passes are available and are more economical. Buses to the more remote corners of the island run infrequently and it is advisable to plan such excursions carefully. Each of the forty walks is preceded by detailed information about bus connections to the starting point. However, changes to the timetable are possible and you are advised to check departure times.

Taxi

Travelling by taxi is of course a more convenient way of seeing the island and fares are relatively cheap. For short distances two people hiring a taxi is often cheaper than travelling by bus. A taxi may be hired for the day and paying for a set time rather than a specified distance can often turn out to be the most economical way of travelling. However, there are times when taking a taxi is the only way of getting to a remote spot. Most taxi drivers can speak a little English and so the fare should be agreed before the journey. Most taxi drivers are prepared to collect passengers from the end of their walk at an agreed time.

All taxis are equipped with meters. A basic charge of is levied for all rides in town and then a charge for each extra kilometre. For longer trips outside Funchal a charge per hour is usual, but charges should be agreed with the driver first.

Car Hire & Driving

Hire cars are an alternative to taxis, but they are certainly not cheap, and for walkers, using a car means that you have to return to your starting point. Furthermore, negotiating local traffic conditions, especially in Funchal, can be a harrowing experience. Drive on the right-hand side of the road. A full driving licence is necessary and seat belts are compulsary.

Roads are in general good, with excellent surfaces and (out of Funchal) little traffic, but they are frequently steep, winding and narrow. There are usually good concrete barriers to protect from steep drops, but drivers should be prepared for journeys which take much longer than expected, as you will seldom be out of first or second gear. One of the few exceptions is the first part of the road across the centre of the island from Ribeira Brava to São Vicente, which is quite level and straight until it climbs steeply over the Encumeada pass. A new motorway bypass is being built around Funchal, with tunnels and spectacular viaducts over the deep valleys, and the above comments do not apply to this and the road to the airport.

A number of minor roads have been, and still are being, upgraded with the help of EC grants. Often you can travel on one of these roads with a new excellent tarmac surface and not meet another vehicle all day!

To Porto Santo
Passenger boats cross regularly to Porto Santo from Funchal harbour (about 1½ hours), with one excursion daily, more frequently in summer, but the crossing can be rough. Special trips are often organised for swimming, fishing or pleasure.

There is also an air service to Porto Santo from Funchal Airport (15 minute flight) with several flights a day.

INDEX

MPC
A Note to the Reader

Thank you for buying this book, we hope it has helped you to plan and enjoy your visit to Madeira. We have worked hard to produce a guidebook which is as accurate as possible. With this in mind, any comments, suggestions or useful information you may have would be appreciated. In particular we would like to know where new road works have affected any of the walks in this book.

Please write to:

The Editor
Moorland Publishing Co Ltd
Moor Farm Road West
Ashbourne
Derbyshire DE6 1HD

The Travel Specialists

Visitor's Guides
Itinerary based guides for independent travellers

MPC

America:
American South West
California
Florida
Orlando & Central
  Florida
USA

Austria:
Austria
Austria: Tyrol &
  Vorarlberg

Britain:
Cornwall & Isles of
  Scilly
Cotswolds
Devon
East Anglia
Hampshire & Isle of
  Wight
Kent
Lake District
Scotland: Lowlands
Somerset, Dorset &
  Wiltshire
North Wales &
  Snowdonia
North York Moors,
  York & Coast
Northern Ireland
Northumbria
Peak District
Treasure Houses of
  England
Yorkshire Dales &
  North Pennines

Canada
Czechoslovakia

Denmark
Egypt

France:
Champagne &
  Alsace-Lorraine
France
Alps & Jura
Brittany
Burgundy &
  Beaujolais
Dordogne
Loire
Massif Central
Normandy
Normandy Landing
  Beaches
Provence & Côte
  d'Azur

Germany:
Bavaria
Black Forest
Northern Germany
Rhine & Mosel
Southern Germany

Greece:
Greece (mainland)
Athens &
  Peloponnese

Holland
Hungary
Iceland & Greenland

India:
Delhi, Agra & Rajasthan
Goa

Ireland

Islands:
Corsica
Crete
Cyprus
Gran Canaria
Guernsey,
  Alderney & Sark
Jersey
Madeira
Mallorca, Menorca,
  Ibiza &
  Formentera
Malta & Gozo
Mauritius, Rodrigues
  & Reunion
Rhodes
Sardinia
Seychelles
Tenerife

Italy:
Florence & Tuscany
Italian Lakes
Northern Italy
Southern Italy

Norway
Peru
Portugal

Spain:
Costa Brava
  & Costa Blanca
Northern & Central
  Spain
Southern Spain
  & Costa del Sol

Sweden
Switzerland
Turkey

MPC Visitor's Guides are available through all good bookshops. Free catalogue available upon request from Moorland Publishing Co Ltd, Moor Farm Rd, Ashbourne, Derbyshire DE6 1HD, England ☎ 01335 344486.

Mail Order In case of local difficulty, you may order direct (quoting your Visa/Access number) from Grantham Book Services on ☎ 01476 67421. Ask for the cash sales department. There is a small charge for postage and packing.

MPC *Visitor's Guides* bring important practical details to your fingertips. Most of them are based upon itineraries, recognising that you may wish to tour around and take in the major places of interest.

Our unique system of symbols readily identify particular features in the text and on the maps. Each chapter finishes with lists of addresses and phone numbers we think may be of help to you. Additionally our Fact File highlights the essential information you need to know about accommodation, currency and credit cards, travel etc.

Our production team works hard to produce user-friendly guides with you in mind. We hope this helps to make your visit more rewarding.

Visitor's Guides are produced in three categories:

 Country Traveller covering particular countries and printed in full colour in a larger format.

 Regional Traveller Printed in a handy pocket size and in full colour. These books cover particular areas or states within a country.

 Holiday Islands Detailed information on far away islands where dreams are made! They are in the same format as the *Regional Traveller* and ideal for packing in your travel bags.

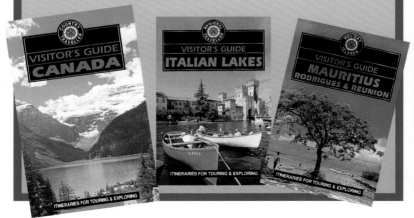